the
way
of
chai

RECIPES FOR A
MEANINGFUL LIFE

the
way
of
chai

kevin wilson

A TarcherPerigee Book

tarcherperigee

An imprint of Penguin Random House LLC
penguinrandomhouse.com

Illustrations by Basak Notz

TarcherPerigee with tp colophon is a registered trademark of Penguin Random House LLC.

Most TarcherPerigee books are available at special quantity discounts for bulk purchase for sales promotions, premiums, fundraising, and educational needs. Special books or book excerpts also can be created to fit specific needs. For details, write SpecialMarkets@penguinrandomhouse.com.

Library of Congress Cataloging-in-Publication Data

Names: Wilson, Kevin, author.
Title: The way of chai: recipes for a meaningful life / Kevin Wilson.
Description: 1. | New York: TarcherPerigee, Penguin Random House LLC, [2023]
Identifiers: LCCN 2023023328 (print) | LCCN 2023023329 (ebook) |
ISBN 9780593538579 (hardcover) | ISBN 9780593538586 (epub)
Subjects: LCSH: Chai tea. | Beverages | Tea. | Cooking (Tea) | LCGFT: Cookbooks.
Classification: LCC TX817.T3 W55 2023 (print) | LCC TX817.T3 (ebook) |
DDC 641.3/372—dc23/eng/20230724
LC record available at https://lccn.loc.gov/2023023328
LC ebook record available at https://lccn.loc.gov/2023023329

Printed in the United States of America
1st Printing

Book design by Shannon Nicole Plunkett

எல்லாப் புகழும் கிறிஸ்துவுக்கே
(All praise be to Christ)

For Sathyanadan Anthony Mathew, my தாத்தா (grandfather).
You toiled in the tea estates so that I could have a better future.
One day I'll tell you what we did, and you won't believe me.

contents

introduction

Setting the Table

I cannot remember my first cup of chai.

This is perhaps because I've been drinking it ever since I could taste things. Having grown up in Sri Lanka, I fondly recall a childhood infused with Ceylon tea—its aromas were symbols of community, hope, and meaning in my life. We called it "thethani"* in my Tamil family, not realizing that it was also known as "chai," "shai," or "cha" in other parts of the world.

Perhaps your first introduction to chai was through Starbucks—the world's largest coffeehouse chain. Maybe you bought this book with the hope that you can finally learn how to make a chai latte in the comfort of your home. Or maybe you grew up with the real thing, and a portion of your internal organs temporarily shuts down every time someone says "chai tea latte."

Or maybe you just looked up "chai" on Amazon, and this piqued your interest.

No matter who you are, thank you for being here.

While etymologically "chai" and "tea" both refer to the same thing (so saying "chai tea" is like saying "tea tea"), the former is typically used to describe the popular South Asian beverage of hospitality, a blend of loose leaf black tea† infused in a base of

---

* "Milk tea" in Tamil. Unless I specify otherwise, I'll use "chai" and "thethani" interchangeably throughout the book to refer to the same beverage.

† Chai is made almost exclusively with black teas. The most common options for chai are Assam CTC (Cut-Tear-Curl) tea, Ceylon BOPF (Broken Orange Pekoe Fannings), or Kenyan BOP (Broken Orange Pekoe).

milk, water, or both, flavored with (or without) aromatic spices, and sweetened with cane sugar or jaggery (the coarse, unrefined brown sugar made in the Indian subcontinent, Southeast Asia, the Caribbean, and Africa by evaporating the sap of palm trees). Chai is a sweet, aromatic, creamy beverage that feels like a hug in a mug. While chai is more commonly known as a South Asian beverage, the spiced milk tea version of it is also consumed in South Central Asia, Southeast Asia, Iran, parts of Africa, and even some parts of Europe.

Within these regions, there is tremendous diversity in how chai is consumed. After speaking to many in the community, I found at least one thing to be clear: There are as many chai recipes as there are families making chai. Each family has its own recipes and unique practices, which they hope to pass on to future generations as a way to preserve their history and legacy. Regardless of how they make it, this drink continues to be an enduring symbol of culture, pride, and heritage for many.

And these families will invite you over for chai . . .

. . . as long as you don't call it "chai tea."

I'm convinced that every time someone says "chai tea," a brown grandma somewhere sheds a silent tear. You wouldn't want that, now, would you?

So now that we're all on the same page, what can you expect from this book?

It's six p.m., right before sunset in a San Diego summer. Picture yourself seated comfortably in the living room of our one-bedroom apartment on my gray IKEA couch that my wife and I assembled four years prior. On your left is a glass door that opens up to a balcony with cactus plants lining the periphery of the metal railing. On a clear day like today, you can see a portion of the Pacific Ocean. The sky above you is slowly transforming itself into a canvas of lilac, yellow, and light blue.

There are cats. Two of them. Leo is an orange and white, half Persian, half Maine Coon ball of floof. Phoebe is a black, god-knows-what breed that we rescued a year ago. Leo is a sweetheart. He drags his furry Garfield-esque body to you for pets. Hope you're not allergic. Phoebe is not so solicitous. She crouches silently in the corner next to our electric piano, blending into its darkness, secretly plotting a thousand ways to take you out. A true menace.

Right in front of you is a small IKEA table with two cups of chai. One for you. One for me. Even if this might be your first time meeting me, you and I are now besteas.

Let me reintroduce myself: I am Kevin Wilson, and I'm somewhat of a cultural "mutt." I was born in Sri Lanka, lived my high school years in Oman, and immigrated to the United States in 2009. Though I'm currently the digital/social media coordinator for my alma mater, Andrews University, I've been an ordained Seventh-day Adventist Christian pastor since 2017. I've been married to my Cuban Chilean American best friend since 2017, although we've known each other since 2009. Life was going predictably slow till February 2020, when my masala chai recipe video went viral on TikTok. My obsession with milk-based teas and chai slowly became public as I kept sharing recipes I liked and stories from my life while making chai. If you still aren't familiar with who I am, or what I sound like, feel free to Google "CrossCultureKev" or "chai guy" or "what does Jesus really look like." Because as you go through this book, I want you to actually picture us discussing these ideas as part of an ongoing chat about our lives, our love for chai, and all the exciting or tumultuous tangents we might encounter as we make our way through the world of chai.

This book is not entirely a recipe book, though every chapter includes a delicious chai recipe that you can make from home and that is inspired by members of our multicultural bestea family.

This book is not entirely a history book, though it interacts with multiple histories.

It's not entirely a self-help book, though it has a collection of ideas that might be helpful to you.

It's not a religious book geared toward a person of the Christian faith or aimed at proselytizing a nonbeliever, though the Way of Jesus might have, intentionally or unintentionally, shaped the ongoing processing of these ideas.

I like to think of this book as a *topography of meaning*, a map of sorts displaying points of interest where you can make pit stops to refresh yourself as you navigate the hills and valleys of your own lived experience.

The following chapters are structured around specific aspects of the chai brewing process in chronological order. Each chapter begins with a chai recipe from my kitchen,* followed by a brief meditation on how a certain facet of chai offers a window into a life that is purposeful, hopeful, and beautiful. In this book, you'll find stories from my own life and other South Asian narratives, which, hopefully, can infuse your life with a little more meaning.

If you're a speed-reader, you may finish this entire book in a couple of hours. Or you may just want to skip to the recipes. Nonetheless, my hope is for you to see these ideas as a gentle encounter with the world and yourself.

I hope each chapter of this book invites you to slow down. To pause. To resist a hurried posture in a hustle-obsessed culture that can often prevent us from savoring the important things, like a cup of homemade chai. And if you haven't already, my hope is that you, too, may begin a love affair with chai.

I hope that these pages offer you a bit of solace amid your struggles, and peace in a world that can feel anything but peaceful, just as a steaming cup of chai smooths out the rough edges of your day.

So grab your cup, bestea.

Unclench your jaw.

Breathe in.

Breathe out.

Sip.

Let's go on a journey.

---

* I may be an expert in how I make chai, but I'm certainly not going to pretend that I know everything about how everyone else does their chai. If there's a chai recipe you're familiar with but that is not included here, after we finish our chat please contact me at crossculturekev.com. That would make my day.

hardware

This is the list of hardware you'll need as you embark on your chai adventure.*

- Liquid measuring cup
- Set of measuring spoons, including teaspoon and tablespoon measures
- 4-inch serrated kitchen knife
- 3½- to 5-inch mortar and pestle set
- 8-ounce long-handled stainless steel ladle
- 1½-quart stainless steel pot with lid
- 3-inch fine-mesh stainless steel strainer
- 12- to 15-ounce frothing pitcher
- 2 mugs that can hold about 1 cup of liquid each
- Electric frother (optional)

---

* For the sake of convenience, all these items are listed in the Amazon store linked on my website, crossculturekev.com. Recipes that require specialty hardware will mention it in those chapters.

CHAPTER 2

terroir

Cultivating a Courageous Character

Darjeeling Chai

Serves 2[*]

INGREDIENTS

½ cup filtered water

2 teaspoons loose leaf Darjeeling tea

2 teaspoons sugar (optional)

2 teaspoons hot full-fat milk (optional)[†]

METHOD

In a medium pot, heat the water over medium-high heat.

When you see small bubbles at the bottom of the pot, turn the heat off and add the tea.[‡]

---

* Every chai recipe in this book is for two servings. One for you. And, ideally, the other for someone else you'd like to share this moment with.

† To make these recipes vegan or dairy-free, simply replace the milk with a plant-based milk option and omit condensed and/or evaporated milk used in other recipes. Full-fat oat milk is a great option. Personally, I've found the flavor of other vegan milk alternatives (soy, almond, rice, coconut, etc.) to conflict with the spices in masala chai. Regardless of what milk you choose, it's vital to go with a thicker milk option (more viscous and full-bodied) rather than a "thin" one.

‡ If you're using an electric stove, remove your pot and place it on a nonheated surface on your stovetop or a heat-resistant surface.

Cover the pot and let the tea steep for 3 to 4 minutes. (If you are not planning to add milk, steep it for 3 minutes.)

Add the sugar and hot milk, if using, and stir till all of the sugar is dissolved. Strain the tea into a pitcher through a fine-mesh strainer.

Serve and enjoy!

He was eleven when he ran away.

After the tragic death of his mother when a kerosene lamp burst into flames during a family gathering on Christmas Eve, this boy and his three toddler siblings were sent to live with his father's brother. In the name of "character development," their uncle forced the boy into hard labor. He would go to school in the morning and come back to a list of chores that would take him the rest of the day to finish.

This went on for months. Unable to keep up with this pace, while also being expected to parent his siblings whenever his father was away working as a கணக்கு பிள்ளை (kanakku pillai),* the boy realized that he needed to find another way to ensure a better future for his family. So in the quiet of the night, he gathered what he could, kissed his siblings goodbye, and jumped on a train headed to the big city.

After a few weeks of surviving on the streets, the boy found employment at a local motel, where he was hired as a peon. He was asked to do everything from waiting on tables and cleaning rooms to running daily errands. By this time, he had made contact with his father and his siblings and even sent a portion of his meager earnings back home to support them. The boy would often dream of the life he wanted to live, the education he wished he had, and the nurture of his late mother. He missed her warm presence,

---

* A supervisor in the tea estates, often a Tamil-speaking Sri Lankan male.

which, before her passing, had felt like a comforting campfire but had since become ambient embers of a bygone flame.

A few more weeks passed. Then a thirty-five-year-old man who'd been staying at the motel noticed the boy and initiated conversation with him. Inspired by the boy's work ethic and communication skills, the man offered him the position of being his research assistant and translator as he worked to complete his doctoral dissertation. The position would involve traveling across the country and having crucial cross-cultural conversations with diverse communities. The boy didn't have anything to lose. He put in his notice, packed the few shirts and shorts he had in his rucksack, and headed out with this man.

For the next five years, the boy and the man covered the farthest corners of the land on a motorcycle. They shared many cups of chai with the locals, and the boy would translate the man's questions into their native tongue and translate their responses back into English. Their friendship blossomed. The boy became the man's only confidant, and the man became the boy's mentor and father figure. This relationship, during the boy's formative years, taught him how to navigate the complexities of life with tact, wisdom, and love. His character developed in ways that he wouldn't realize until much later.

When the man's research was done, it was time for him to leave the country. The man knew that when he left, the boy would, at best, be back in the motel, or, at worst, be back on the streets doing odd jobs to make a living.

The man knew what he had to do.

He found the best school in town and met with the principal. "I know his record isn't great, but he's a hard worker," he said in an attempt to convince the principal. The man then took out his notepad, scribbled some figures, and handed it to him. "Here's my account information. Please contact me if he needs financial support for anything. From here on out, I'm his sponsor."

The man and the boy shopped for dorm supplies, making sure that the boy had everything he needed for the first few months of school. During their last few days together, they laughed, cried, and shared memories from their adventures and escapades. Right before the man's departure, they shared one last tearful embrace, not knowing when or if they would ever see each other again.

Little did the boy know, however, that they would meet again ...

... thirty-five years later.

If you want to, you can skip to the end of this chapter to find out what happened to the boy. But stay with me for a bit, bestea.

The particular social situations, life experiences, and interpersonal relationships that led to the turning point in the boy's life remind me of the varied factors that have to come together to make a good cup of chai. The best place to start as we embark on this multisensory experience is to begin with the first, and perhaps most important, of those factors: its "terroir."

Simply put, the terroir of chai encompasses the natural

conditions of tea growth, including topography, soil composition, climate, and cultivation methods. Before your chai ever touches your tongue, its flavors have already been determined by factors beyond your knowledge or control.

In Sri Lanka, for instance, there are four different types of tea that are produced from a single plant—*Camellia sinensis*—each of them inheriting a specific flavor profile based on the elevation at which it was grown.* රත් වත්ත (Ran watte) tea is grown at around six thousand feet above sea level, producing a fine, subtle, mellow tea similar to the consistency of fine wine. උඩ වත්ත (Uda watte) tea is cultivated at about five thousand feet above sea level, creating a well-rounded tea with a rich aroma. මැද වත්ත (Madha watte) tea is grown around three thousand feet above sea level and is heavier and full-bodied. Finally, යට වත්ත (Yata watte) tea is grown at only one thousand feet above sea level to create an intense, strong tea.

Different soil compositions of tea estates affect tea quality as well. The nutrients processed through the metabolic reactions of tea plants produce different flavors depending on where they are grown. Ran watte tea is a fine tea not only because of the cooler climate in which it is grown but also because of the claylike composition of the up-country hills. The lower you go, all the way down to Yata watte tea, the sandier the soil becomes, which causes the teas to be bolder and more earthy.

---

* Edwin Soon, *The Dilmah Way of Tea* (Peliyagoda, Sri Lanka: Ceylon Tea Services, 2009).

Driving through பொகவந்தலாவை (Bogawantalawa), the village where my father was born, always takes my breath away. It's as if God shades the lush plantations of the tea estates with clouds, causing parts of it to glow with a verdant iridescence while dimming others to form a symphony of color. Such factors like cloud formation and the intensity and luminosity of the sun affect the flavors of tea. Each tea estate, then, can produce different varieties of tea within their unique flavor profiles simply because of where the clouds landed. "Shaded" teas become finer, while those exposed to consistent sunlight become earthier.

A discussion of tea terroir would be incomplete without the mention of Darjeeling chai. Grown at an elevation of 6,700 feet in the Darjeeling region of West Bengal, India, Darjeeling tea is considered the champagne of teas. In the same way that no other whiskey can be labeled "Scotch" unless it's made in Scotland, or no other tangy cheese should be named "Cheddar" unless it comes from the Cheddar district in England, no other tea should be named "Darjeeling" unless it comes from Darjeeling. The fact that it's the first product of India to be accredited with GI[*] status is due to various factors, including Darjeeling's specific ecological conditions that cannot be replicated elsewhere, the low yield

---

* Geographical indication; a designation for products that have a clear link between the product and its place of origin.

of the Darjeeling leaf that accounts for only 1 percent of India's tea production, and the amount of labor that goes into maintaining and cultivating this fine tea. It's a black tea that appears as "white" or "green"—less astringent than black tea but more complex than green.

Additionally, the different seasons in which Darjeeling chai is harvested yield what tea connoisseurs describe as "flushes." Plucked between mid-March and April, following the dormancy of the Himalayan winter, the first leaves of the tea plant produce a tea that is light and floral. Second-flush teas are picked between May and June, producing teas that are brighter, full-bodied, and fruitier. Within two weeks of the second flush, the "muscatel" teas arrive, developing their winelike flavors as a result of insects that feed on the leaves. During that short window, the *Empoasca*, a species of grasshopper, and the *Homona coffearia*, a type of moth, breed on the tea leaves and chew on them, causing a chemical reaction that oxidizes the leaves, which concentrates their flavors and aromas within the plant even before they are processed at the factory. Only the right combination of ecological conditions, animal behavior, and careful factory processing can qualify a batch of second-flush Darjeeling as muscatel. The third-flush, or monsoon-flush, teas are picked during the heavy showers between July and September and are best used in blends and tea bags because of their high moisture content. The fourth and final flush is harvested from October to November, producing teas with a heavy brasslike liquor that are more astringent and full-bodied than previous flushes.

Whether it's the different flushes of Darjeeling chai, Ceylon tea from the various regions of Sri Lanka, or any other tea harvested to make chai, they couldn't have made it into your cup without the power, place, and permission of their terroir.

That's why when you taste tea, you also taste its nature. You taste fruitiness and fresh hills. You taste sweetness and sunlight. You taste richness and rain.

Each sip is not only an infusion of complex flavors but a distillation of different ecologies.

Character—the inner, subterranean foundations of an individual that empower them to navigate the ebb and flow of being human—can in many ways be described as the terroir of the soul. It is the unique coalescence of one's moral ecology, cultural history, and responses to the vicissitudes of life. The tea estates, I believe, can point us to at least two conditions for cultivating the good life, which I define as a life that is fruitful, flavorful, and flourishing amid fluctuating seasons.

First, character is formed by our commitments. The word "commitment" comes from the Latin root "mittere," which means "to release." This captures the essence of any commitment—in contrast to a contract—because a commitment involves letting go of control in order to develop a new dynamic that can only work with the free and full cooperation of its participants. Whether tea plants have the freedom to release control, or some form of agency to choose their responses, it is evident that, at some foundational level, they have to make certain commitments with their terroir to ensure the survival of their species. I can almost imagine the plant having a conversation with herself: *When are you going to absorb the nutrients from the soil? Are you going to photosynthesize now or later? What's your process for oxidizing the leaves?* Good character, like good chai, is a by-product of this inner dialogue between who we are and who we want to be.

The importance of releasing control is even clearer among us humans. Elynn and I have to release a fair bit of control in order to make our marriage work. A parent must learn to loosen their expectations in order to envision new possibilities for their children. A teacher must learn to relax their hold on student outcomes so that students can grow, even beyond the limits of standardization. Any commitment worth pursuing, any relationship worth improving, has to involve a periodic release of what you think *should* be so that you can begin to recognize the varied possibilities of what *could* be. This way, the commitments you have made, and will make, will continue to galvanize your character and shape the person you're becoming.

The seeds of commitment flourish in the soil of love. When you make and keep a promise based on your love for yourself and for the one you're committing to, the mutual work that goes into cultivating the relationship, with all its highs, lows, ups, and downs, can transform the promise into a lush garden of relational bliss that bears fruit in season and out of season. Every commitment you keep, either to yourself or to someone else, fertilizes your being and expands its capacity to receive and give more. But this same garden can wither and grow weeds when the love that once nourished it is misunderstood, exploited, or abused. We feel it at a soul level, down in the strata of our beings, when these commitments are broken. This is why it's important to choose your commitments wisely. Just because you can doesn't mean you should.

You have agency, bestea.

Second, character is forged by our confrontations. When free agents within a system relate to each other, there is always going to be a fair bit of resistance whenever diverse viewpoints clash. Freedom presupposes risk, and risk invites confrontation. And care-full confrontation, if we allow it to be, could be a way of interacting with the world that goes beyond pleasantries and gets at the heart of the matter. It can be a posture of being that respects the dignity and capacity of both the confronter and the one being confronted. The fact that confrontation is often activated by things like trauma, anger, or frustration is a testament to the difficulty of fully encountering the "other" in a culture here in the West that often conditions us to be mile-wide but inch-deep in our interactions with the world.

The terroir of tea, however, will remind us of the beauty and the blessing of confrontations that are carried out with care, love, and knowledge of what we're achieving together. After the monsoon showers, the tea plants have to confront the waterlogged soil in order to draw the right amount of moisture into their leaves. During seasons of high heat, the cell organelles within the leaves have to communicate with each other to ensure adequate nourishment of the leaves. Insects like the *Empoasca* force the plants to respond, creating rare flavors of chai during a very short window of time. The calloused hands of the tea-plucking ராணி (rani)*—the woman who works tirelessly in the estates from dawn to dusk—reveal her confrontations with the terroir of the land and the terroir of the workers' lives. The same hand that often curls up into an angry fist because of unjust, unethical practices in their work is the same hand that opens to pluck the tea leaves so that their children can have a better future. The leaves, their pluckers, and their terroir exist in a complex relationship with one another, each doing their best to ensure both the vitality and the perpetuity of chai. Saturated in every sip, then, is a series of confrontations, without which chai becomes nothing more than a comforting beverage on a cold afternoon.

What are you confronting right now? What are you contending against during this season of your life?

Maybe it's something at your job. Maybe it's a problem that needs to be solved. Maybe it's a relationship that you know is good for you and nourishes you, but you didn't expect the friction. Maybe it's injustice. Maybe it's being aware of the ways people have been marginalized, either by the state or by bad religion. Maybe it's the difficulty and the loneliness of taking steps toward

---

* "Queen" in Tamil.

reconciliation, fairness, and equality, engaging with those who have been hurt.

Or maybe it's you. Maybe it's confronting the person you have become. Maybe it's confronting the person you thought you would become. Maybe it's coming face-to-face with your person, either in your therapist's office, behind closed doors during your devotional time, or through the lens of someone else. Maybe it's working on aspects of yourself that are wounded, fractured, and in need of healing.

Whatever it is, my bestea, I want to remind you that as long as you have breath in your lungs, and a beat to your heart, the confrontations of your life will always be reordering, recalibrating, and reengineering your inner being. If you have a chance to peer into it, instead of seeing a terribly tattered rag stained by pain, you'll see a tapestry of character, woven by strength. Look at where you are now. Probably not the place you wanted to be, or the person you thought you'd be. But I like to think that it is not where you used to be. You've changed. You're changing. It's hard to notice that you're healing *when* you're healing. What you've experienced, and are experiencing, has made you stronger, kinder, and braver than you admit.

If you have confronted this season, and everything that has come with it, what can't you do?

Your commitments are forming you.

Your confrontations are forging you.

And this brings us back to the story that started this chapter.

After Rob,[*] the man who had helped the boy, left to return to California to finish his dissertation at UCLA, the boy focused his energies in school, a place that he'd not been in for over a decade. His school day began at three a.m. every day, when he would spend the first few hours before dawn milking the cows in the school dairy and feeding the chickens at the poultry farm before rushing to his classes. After years of confronting his difficulties and consistently committing to building a better future for himself, the boy managed to graduate and was accepted to a nursing school in Pakistan.

Somewhere between receiving his college diploma and nursing credentials, he met a kind, beautiful, resilient woman and fell in love with her. They got engaged at the university where they were both students. After five years, they returned to their home country and got married.

They would go on to have two children. The younger one, a girl, was named Khayali. The older one, a boy, they named Kevin.

Kevin Wilson.

The boy who was now fully grown was none other than my dada—my father.

In the summer of 2014, Dada came to the United States for the first time to attend my college graduation. While the main reason why he'd saved up was to celebrate his son, he was also hoping to accomplish one more thing: to see Rob after all these years.

---

[*] Not his actual name.

So we scoured the internet. We tried to contact him. After days of searching and planning and sifting through many Robs, we got an address. He didn't live too far away.

Dada and I drove to his house, which was perched on top of a hill, overlooking the beautiful hills near Pasadena, California. I didn't know if he had done it on purpose, but we knew it was the place because walking toward the main door felt like walking into a dense jungle, unsurprisingly similar to the lush greenery of my hometown, கண்டி (Kandy)—a place Dada and Rob would have frequented during their many adventures.

We knocked on the door and were greeted by the sweet smile of a man probably in his late seventies.

"Hi? How can I help y—" His voice cut off when he saw my father a few feet behind me.

"Wilson?"

"Rob! It's me!" Dada said as he rushed past me, almost tripping me over. Dada hugged Rob so tightly that I got nervous that this might be Rob's last embrace with another human.

Rob invited us into his living room, which I can only describe as organized chaos filled with books, memorabilia, and trinkets from his travels. I moved my chair slightly away from both of them, wondering if they needed more space to catch up on the past few decades of their lives. I didn't say a word. I just listened and tried to hold back tears as I witnessed Dada and Rob shape-shift into their younger selves—giddy, wide-eyed, brave adventurers—reliving their motorcycle diaries of Sri Lanka.

Rob and Dada are among the best humans I know. But they didn't get to where they are today and become the kinds of people they are just because of sheer agency. They didn't grow *in spite* of their circumstances; they grew *from* them. Their characters were a result of not just intention and determination but also how they contended with the unique terroirs of their lives. Rob confronted the difficulties of being in a different culture and made a commitment to be present for his friend, a friendship that has not only blessed Dada but every generation that has and will come after him. Dada confronted the difficulties of his childhood and the trauma of his past while committing to create a better future for his family than the one he had experienced as a kid in the tea estates. The love and nurture that he didn't receive as a little boy, he now experiences through his commitment to his family.

My bestea, as you sip your tea today and think about where your chai came from, my prayer is that you will see your life not as a linear progression toward uncertainty but as an arboretum of possibility.

May you see the passage of time not as a cruel inevitability but as a wild yet abundant landscape filled with confrontations and commitments—a terroir of opportunity.

CHAPTER 3

leaf

Steeping in Empathy

Sri Lankan Lemon Tea

Serves 2

INGREDIENTS

3 green cardamom pods

1 cup filtered water

1 teaspoon fresh crushed ginger

1½ teaspoons loose leaf Ceylon BOPF[*] black tea

1 cup full-fat milk[†]

4 teaspoons sugar

METHOD

Crush the cardamom with a mortar and pestle and set aside.

In a medium pot, heat the water over medium-high heat.

When you see small bubbles at the bottom of the pot, add the crushed cardamom and ginger.

---

[*] Broken Orange Pekoe Fannings, the main grade of tea in Sri Lanka.

[†] In Sri Lanka, full-fat evaporated milk powder is often used instead of liquid milk. If you use milk powder, I recommend 3 tablespoons of milk powder with 2 cups of filtered water instead. Use the same method as in the Sri Lankan thethani recipe in the following chapter.

When the water comes to a vigorous boil, stir the tea into the water.

Turn the heat down to low and cover the pot. Steep the tea for 1 minute.

Uncover the pot and add the milk. Turn the heat up to high. Stir the tea for a few minutes, then let it steep undisturbed with the cover off.

When the tea rises to the top of the pot, turn the heat off and stir in the sugar till all of it is dissolved.

Strain the tea into a pitcher through a fine-mesh strainer. Aerate the tea by transferring it between the pot and the pitcher a few times or by using an electric frother.

Serve and enjoy!

t is the summer of 2011.

I am sitting cross-legged on a beautiful carpet with bright, intricate calligraphy that spreads across the entire floor of the largest room I've ever been in. Magnificent, tiered chandeliers hang gracefully from a ceiling so high that everyone in the room seems like ants, Lilliputian in comparison, attempting to access a larger world.

I am the only one seated where I am. Everyone else is about twenty feet away from me, standing and exchanging pleasantries with one another. After a few minutes, I hear a beautiful male tenor voice bellowing in Arabic through large speakers. The music, a melodic sequence I heard five times a day when I was a teenager in Oman, embraces me like a close friend would after serendipitously meeting me in a crowd of strangers. I know what is going to happen next.

They are going to pray.

It's not every day that a Christian like myself frequents a mosque, let alone a mosque in North Sudan. But I have traveled from Michigan, where I am still a sophomore in college at the time, to be here for an auspicious occasion: the Nikah ceremony of one of my best friends, Naushad, a Sri Lankan Muslim, who's about to sign the marriage contract after a prayer of consecration in the presence of witnesses and the representatives of Arwa, his bride. This is a very intimate ceremony with close male family and friends, to which I, one of his groomsmen, have also been invited.

As the congregants gather, I remember the tea I had just the day prior. Enam, the bride's sister, prepared a Sudanese ginger and mint tea as a welcome beverage for Naushad's family and friends on their first visit to the bride's house. As she gracefully poured the tea into small, ornate glass cups—the type of cups that you only bring out for special occasions—I felt a sense of disappointment creeping within me.

It's a green tea, I thought.

Except it wasn't. "Green tea" was my ignorant catchall categorization for any teas that are light teas, including this one that was more red than green. I've never liked "green" teas. Maybe because they are too "thin." Maybe because they taste like how "leaf sweat" would taste. Maybe because my palate's gotten used to full-bodied, bold, creamy-textured drinks like a Sri Lankan தேத்தண்ணி (thethani).* Or maybe because I'm just not sophisticated enough.

With the polite smile I've rehearsed for times like this, I reluctantly reached out to receive the cup with both hands from Enam. It was piping hot, with a temperature only a few degrees cooler than Khartoum. I brought the cup to my lips and gently tilted it toward me. I blew gently through my teeth to cool my first sip and pulled the liquid into my mouth, lightly aerating it in the process.

I was shook.

This was one of the best tea experiences I've had.

---

* "Milk tea" in Tamil; also called කිරි තේ (kiri té) in Sinhala.

"Sweet heat" is how I would describe the initial taste as the first sip sloshed around in my mouth. As it made its way into my body, the heat was soon replaced by a chill from the mint. For a moment, I forgot we were in North Africa as the light steam from the chai caressed my forehead, cooling my skin the way it cooled my insides. The aftertaste was sublime—gingery, caramelly notes awakened as if we were in a gentle winter.

The families, cultures, and stories that coalesced into a shared experience over this chai remind me of the interconnectedness of tea. Most horticulturists and food historians agree that although tea is cultivated in many parts of the world and serves different functions, all tea ultimately comes from the same species, *Camellia sinensis*. This means that whether your tea is black, oolong, white, green, or pu-erh, all of them find their origins in this one species. The differences, then, between the teas are a result of many factors, including but not limited to which parts of the leaves are plucked, when they are plucked, how they are processed, how much they are oxidized, and how they are brewed.

Chai may be diverse in its history, but it is similar in its biology.

According to some anthropologists, indigenous tea trees were first discovered by prehistoric humans on their foraging quests. After observing wild animals chewing on the leaves, they started using tea leaves as edibles to give them energy boosts throughout the day.[*] Once they learned how to use fire to brew stews, they figured out how to use tea to supplement their various concoctions. This knowledge of tea spread for the next centuries, and by the time of the Shang Dynasty (1766–1050 BCE), tea was also used for its medicinal properties.

Over time, tea has become a transcultural, global drink that continues to unite different cultures, experiences, and stories. A construction worker sipping kadak chai[†] in Dubai, a boy rushing into the kitchen after smelling his amma's[‡] kiri té in Colombo, a business executive in Hong Kong about to take his first sip of milk tea of the day, and some Sri Lankans and North Africans sharing a cup of ginger and mint tea are somehow inextricably bound to each other through a single drink. Thus, for thousands of years, the second most consumed beverage on the planet[§] has presented itself as an enduring connector of humanity.

In his notable commencement address at Oberlin College in 1965, Reverend Dr. Martin Luther King Jr. describes this interconnectedness:

All mankind is tied together, all life is interrelated, and we are all caught in an inescapable network of mutuality, tied in a

---

[*] Mary Lou Heiss and Robert J. Heiss, *The Story of Tea: A Cultural History and Drinking Guide* (Berkeley, CA: Ten Speed Press, 2007), 6.

[†] "Strong tea" in Hindi.

[‡] "Mom" in Tamil and Sinhala.

[§] Water is the first. Crazy.

*single garment of destiny. Whatever affects one directly, af-
fects all indirectly. For some strange reason I can never be
what I ought to be until you are what you ought to be. And you
can never be what you ought to be until I am what I ought to
be—this is the interrelated structure of reality.* *

A high inflection in the tenor voice interrupts my daydream-
ing about Enam's tea.

The imam[†] has called everyone to prayer by reciting words
from the Holy Qur'an. People of different ages and stature and
from various walks of life line up next to each other and orient
their bodies in different positions of prayer. It is holy, synchro-
nous, and beautiful. After the prayer, the people sit cross-legged
on the floor next to each other for the wedding ceremony. The
imam gives a brief sermon and then faces the wedding party to
share his invocation. No sooner do they sign the contract and
exchange gifts than a hug fest ensues. Witnessing a complete
disregard of personal space as they kiss one another's cheeks
and tightly embrace each other, I oddly yet unsurprisingly feel
warm and nostalgic—a bit envious, even—as I recall how my
sister, Khayali, and I were loved by our சித்திகள் (chithis),[‡]

---

* Martin Luther King Jr., "Remaining Awake through a Great Revolution"
(commencement address, Oberlin College, June 1965), https://www2.oberlin.edu
/external/eog/blackhistorymonth/mlk/commaddress.html.

† A Muslim leader who leads prayers in a mosque and who is often the spiritual guide
in that particular community of faith.

‡ "Aunts" in Tamil; our mom's sisters.

மாமிகள் (māamis),* சிச்தப்பாமார் (sithappas),† and மாமாக்கள்
(māmas),‡ the memories slowly escaping from the enclosures I
had built using the scaffoldings of American appropriateness
and Western respectability.

Should I approach them? I wonder.

*Is it even okay for me, a cultural and religious outsider, to join
their love mosh pit?*

I am hoping Naushad will stop hugging people and rescue me
from being an awkward bystander when a tall, strong Sudanese
man in his thirties moves out of the crowd into the open and
calls out to me:

"Come, my friend!"

Now I am panicking.

I reluctantly inch my way toward him with a half smile, trying
to hide my anxiety. I have barely taken a few steps when at least
ten members of the family see me and rush in my direction.

Welp. I guess we're doing this, I think as I embrace what is
about to happen:

Beards.

Hugs.

Stubble.

Kisses.

---

* "Aunts" in Tamil; our dad's sisters.

† "Uncles" in Tamil; our dad's brothers.

‡ "Uncles" in Tamil; our mom's brothers.

Bukhoor.*

Arabic.

It is so glorious, I cry. Because I feel seen. I feel known. I'm not an outsider but an insider who has just arrived. Neither language nor culture can prevent our stories from converging, even for that moment, forming a core memory shaped by their empathy.

In a post-pandemic age, attempting to navigate between the extremes of individualism on one end and tribalism on the other, I am convinced that our flourishing depends on how well we answer, and live out, the age-old question first presented by Rabbi Yeshua of Nazareth, which was later contextualized for a younger audience by Pastor Fred Rogers:

"Who is your neighbor?"

For the extent that we see our destinies interwoven with each other in the human family is the extent to which we can create spaces for mutual belonging and unconditional acceptance in a world that often doesn't know it needs them. Choosing empathy means choosing to consider the perspectives and pain of others so that you can understand them better. Empathy means orienting yourself toward their being, a courageous act that builds a bridge of meaning between you and them upon which stories can be explored in nonthreatening, life-giving ways. Contrary to popular belief, empathy is not about imagining what it's like to "walk in someone else's shoes." Rather, true empathy is about

---

* A type of fragrance found in Muslim communities that is used during special occasions. Often used to freshen up interiors, it also is passed onto guests to scent their clothes and hair.

choosing to listen to someone else recount what it's like to walk in their shoes and to trust their story even when it may not match or agree with your experience. True empathy is recognizing that you can never be an expert in someone else's story.

By helping you consider the lived experiences of others, the practice of empathy also allows you to understand yourself more. When you are in the presence of an "other"—someone who lives, loves, or sees differently than you do—and are outside of your own internal chatter, even for a bit, you are moved to revisit your own assumptions about the world and how it should function.

However, empathy is not endorsement. Attention does not always mean approval. Listening does not always mean license. Compassion does not have to mean compromise. Just because you're merciful to someone does not mean that you now have to agree with everything they say or do. It just means that in that moment, and for many moments after that, you have chosen to orient yourself to the needs of someone other than yourself without any conditions for your compassion.

I believe chai is empathy in liquid form. Authentic chai is the type of beverage that invites one to step into a slow process of knowing rather than into a fast, consumptive experience that is more focused on the drinking at the expense of the sharing. The first sip of homemade chai should sensitize you to the reality that what you're about to drink isn't just an exotic beverage but an elixir of experiences. Everything that goes into a reputable, high-quality chai blend, including its leaves, is a product of real lives and stories coming together to create a singular moment of absorption that can expand one's capacity to understand, and even celebrate, narratives that are different from their own. To experience chai, to honor its rituals, to celebrate its heritage, and to enjoy its cultures is to steep in empathy—a patient practice of unconditional love rooted in nothing other than the dignity and the humanity of the communities that have birthed it.

A few hours later, I am at a different location for the wedding ceremony. Naushad and Arwa are married, and the celebrations are still going on. I'm tired, but in a good way, as I pause for a juice break. As I take a few sips, I notice an older gentleman whom I vaguely recognize as an uncle of Arwa's slowly walking toward me. I smile, acknowledging him, and turn toward the direction of the stage to look at a music performance that has been going on. But he keeps walking toward me with a face that looks like he has something important to say.

"Hi, Uncle! How is the wed—" Before I can finish my sentence, he places his calloused, firm hands on my shoulders as if to pull me into an embrace.

I feel his grip tighten, almost to the point of discomfort. He brings me close toward his wise, wrinkled face.

"I want you . . . become Muslim . . ." he growls.

"I want you . . . become Muslim . . . because . . ."

He isn't done. He is simply ramping up for what he has come to really say, which is what I want to leave you with at this point in our journey.

Something I know but forget at times, even as a follower of Christ. The basis for any meaningful posture toward the "other." The foundational truth that can shift an "us versus them" mentality to an "us for them" mindset in a polarized world. The condition for true empathy.

The phrase I want you, my bestea, to believe for yourself, and believe about others, as you sip your chai today.

". . . I love you."

CHAPTER 4

labor

Thriving in Gratitude Mode

Sri Lankan Thethani (Kiri Té)

Serves 2

INGREDIENTS

- 1 teaspoon fresh crushed ginger

- 2 cups filtered water

- 1½ teaspoons loose leaf Ceylon BOPF black tea

- 3 generous tablespoons sweetened condensed milk,
  OR 2 tablespoons full-fat evaporated milk powder
  plus 3 teaspoons sugar

METHOD

Crush the ginger with a mortar and pestle till it disintegrates into small bits and set aside.

In a medium pot, heat the water over medium heat.

When you see small bubbles at the bottom of the pot, add the crushed ginger and the tea.

When the water comes to a rolling boil, turn the heat off and cover the pot. Steep the tea for 3 minutes.

Meanwhile, put the sweetened condensed milk (or milk powder and sugar) in a small pitcher.

Strain the tea into the pitcher through a fine-mesh strainer. Stir until all the ingredients are fully combined.

Aerate the tea by transferring it between the pot and the pitcher a few times or by using an electric frother.

Serve and enjoy!

A re you serious?" I'd lash out at Dada whenever he said that we were going to Kotagala, the village where my தாத்தா (thaatha)* used to live. As a nine-year-old kid who had a rather cushy life compared to many of his friends and cousins, I loathed going to a place where I wouldn't have access to TV, cartoons, or dial-up internet to download the latest pop songs from LimeWire (if you know, you know).

But that was not all.

Going to Kotagala meant that I would have to use the dreaded outhouse.

Instead of a commode and a flush connected to running water, my grandfather had a one-person squat latrine located a few feet away from the house that was fortified using a mixture of pitch and cow dung.

As its name suggests, every time you used a squat latrine, you'd be getting a leg workout in addition to a sweet release. Using it, especially after dark, was also like embarking on a suspenseful adventure where you had no idea what new creatures you were going to encounter lurking in the dark. Perhaps that was why Thaatha, an avid animal lover, didn't pay for the cable subscription of the Discovery Channel; he encountered live wildlife every time he used the bathroom. The cherry on top of this outhouse experience was the visitation of God's greatest mistake: mosquitoes. You just had

---

* "Grandfather" in Tamil.

to prayerfully make sure that the bug swatting during your business didn't knock you off your precarious position or, worse, cause you to swat at places that'd fill you with instant regret.

Growing up, my sister, Khayali, and I were shielded from the poverty and inequality felt by many throughout the island, including those of the tea plantation workers—a demographic that my thaatha was a part of. On the way to his house, I remember seeing women dressed in beautiful saris, donning large sacks on their backs, spread out across the lush landscape, picking tea leaves. From a distance, the hills looked alive with colorful shifting spots, the laborers' arms moving to and from the tea bushes, deftly snapping "two leaves and a bud" for finer teas and "three leaves and a bud" for more common ones. If you were close enough, you could even hear them hum a tune in unison—their melodic Tamil songs lightening the tedium of the work and perhaps also offering much-needed distraction from the pain of their lacerated fingers.

Women were employed as tea pluckers by the early colonists to conserve the male labor force for more demanding work, and also, given that women were paid far less, it was a no-brainer for the planters to choose women to fuel the first rung in their imperial chai production engine.[*] Let us, for a moment, step into the

---

[*] Piya Chatterjee, *A Time for Tea: Women, Labor and Post/Colonial Politics on an Indian Plantation* (New Delhi: Zubaan, 2003).

shoes of a tea plucker in Sri Lanka today. Before the crack of dawn, she congregates with fellow pluckers at a meeting point close to the tea factory. The small talk is cut short when the supervisor assigns her and a few of her friends to a specific location on the plantation. Upon entering her harvesting zone, she wastes no time. With careful, rhythmic precision, she begins to nip the top leaves of the tea plants and throw them into her sack. She has to make two or three trips to the weighing station, where her harvest is weighed and registered by the supervisor. She usually has slippers on, but sometimes rushes out without them when she gets delayed by preparing breakfast for her family of five. It doesn't bother her. Occasionally working barefoot over the years has calloused her feet and desensitized them to the rocky plantation terrain.

In order to earn a daily wage of about 900 rupees ($2.79 USD), she has to collect a minimum of 18 kilograms (40 pounds) of tender green tea leaves. It takes two thousand to four thousand stems to make a single kilogram of tea, which, depending on the type of tea produced after factory processing, yields about 215 grams (7½ ounces) of chai. As the sun goes down, she takes her last sackful to the supervisor, who weighs it. Normally she's confident about her collection, but today she's slightly nervous. Sivalakshmi, her best friend and neighbor, has a broken finger from husking a coconut a few days ago, which has impeded her ability to meet her quota today. At a safe distance from the weighing station, outside the purview of the supervisor, she surreptitiously dropped a few handfuls of tea into Sivalakshmi's duffel.

While her bag is on the hook, she starts to internally panic as the supervisor looks sternly at her. She needs the money. She cannot afford to go through another night of facing her husband's alcoholic rage at not bringing enough home. She needs to get groceries for her kids' meals this week.

Her pulse quickens.

The supervisor breaks the anxious silence. "சரி, இந்தா" ("Sari, indha"; "You're good. Here"), he grunts as he hands over a wad of rupees.

She's made it. She'll be back tomorrow.

Even though I disliked going to Kotagala, I tried to make the most of my time by playing with the kids my age on the tea estates—the children of the tea pluckers. I remember feeling uneasy because I often had better clothing or toys than they did, and I didn't want them to feel bad. But it was only a matter of time until those thoughts disappeared because my friends never seemed to notice. They were perennially happy. Pure joy emanated from them as they found new ways to play with old toys. I recall my frustrations and petty grievances fading away in the presence of their unadulterated bliss, even if it was for a moment.

How? How could they be so joyful in the midst of their challenging lifestyles, which, to a spoiled city brat like me, sounded like a nightmare?

I think I got a glimpse into this mystery on one particular visit to Kotagala when I was around eleven—my last visit with my thaatha before he passed away. During small talk with one of his neighbors, a tea plantation worker, I asked her how she was able to stay joyful despite the difficulties that her family was going through.

I'll never forget what she said:

"தம்பி [thambi],* this is our reality. This is what we've been given. We are thankful for what we have while we face what's in front of us. This brings us joy."

This attitude toward gratitude, while commonplace in settings like Sri Lanka and India—places where people are used to living under oppressive regimes, unreliable governments, and economic instability—is markedly different compared to how it is in the West. When I was eighteen, during my first year as an immigrant to the United States, one of the cultural norms that surprised me was seeing how gratitude was practiced and promoted primarily as a "mood"—an acute "kind-consciousness" that was nurtured, particularly during certain events like Thanksgiving. I remember being baffled by how many people emphasized the importance of doing thoughtful services toward others and cultivating a thankful mindset, only to break through mall-door barricades less than twenty-four hours later to snag limited Black Friday deals.

In contrast, for this woman and other tea plantation workers facing similar difficulties, gratitude was less of a "mood" and more

---

* "Younger brother" in Tamil.

of a "mode": a way of being informed by a higher story than what their experiences were capable of telling. Gratitude, for them, was a deep posture of the heart, reinforced by the belief that there was more to their lives than what they could see, touch, and feel. This attitude, to be sure, is not to be confused with apathy or passivity. The ongoing protests against exploitative practices in tea plantations across South Asia and the continual petitions to offer better living conditions to workers reveal that gratitude can, and should, coexist with justice. Justice without gratitude becomes harsh. Gratitude without justice becomes hollow.

So I'm not inviting you to be thankful or grateful in that vague, Pinterest-y, chai-mug-aesthetic type of way. The labor that goes into the thethani in your cup and the stories of resilience from the tea estates remind us that gratitude is far too complex, too precious, and too necessary a life orientation to be reduced to a mere platitude.

But I invite you, bestea, to consider adopting gratitude as a life "mode" that permeates all of your being rather than an emotional "mood" that affects just some of it sometimes. Just like a home-made cup of chai, this will only happen with deliberate and consistent intention. For me, this mode is activated at the beginning of the day during my meditative time, when I choose to internalize that I'm part of a higher story than what my sensory or experiential inputs are telling me. The degree to which I choose to believe this, regardless of the challenges I might face that day, is the degree to which this mode is sustained.

What happens when you're on gratitude mode? You begin to

view career success not just vertically but also horizontally, not just concerned with how high you can go but also about how many you can take with you on your way there.

When you're on gratitude mode, leaving a legacy becomes less about how you may rise and more about who you can raise.

When you're on gratitude mode, you begin to notice the human behind the hustle. You begin to have a broader view of others. You begin to measure others' worth not just by what they do but also by who they are *while* they do it and who they are *after* they do it. You become sensitized to their capacity for gratitude, which increases your empathy for them.

When you're on gratitude mode, you become a person of justice. The awareness of the dignity of others, activated through your practice of gratitude, will often make you more alert to when they are treated unjustly. Your heart begins to break because of the things that break others. As your life grows deeper in gratitude, it tends to grow wider in compassion. Gratitude is no longer a passive emotion but becomes a restorative force, an existential protest of your being no less brave or bold than the protests of today.

I think of going back to the plantations, hopefully now with a perspective slightly larger than when I was a petty middle schooler. I wish I could turn back time and have all four limbs on the wet up-country dirt with my thaatha, unfazed that his white சாரம் (sāram)* is going to require a strenuous scrub in the local river as

---

* Garment tied around the waist by Tamil-speaking men in Sri Lanka.

he shows me the latest new bug he's found in his backyard. I wish to spend more time with the neighbors' kids and ask their parents more questions.

In the meantime, I'll remind you and myself that gratitude can be a posture of resistance against disappointment, anxiety, and despair.

Gratitude can be a posture of revolution against mediums of instant gratification intent on monetizing our restlessness by offering quick and empty alternatives to a meaningful life.

Gratitude, founded on an unshakable core, galvanized by other-oriented love, is a way of life that detoxifies the self, expands your being, and humanizes your labor.

So next time you sip your chai, I hope you realize, bestea, that the beauty of that moment was shaped by the labor of those who came before you. And as the chai slowly becomes a part of you, may you explore the possibility that yours is not a single, solitary story, isolated and on its own. You are part of a larger saga that is richer with yours in it.

CHAPTER 5

drying

Living in the Liminal Space

South African Rooibos Chai

Caffeine-Free

Serves 2

INGREDIENTS

3 green cardamom pods

1 (1-inch) cinnamon stick

2 peppercorns

2 cloves (optional)

1 cup filtered water

2 teaspoons loose leaf rooibos tea

1 teaspoon fresh crushed ginger

1 cup full-fat milk

2 to 3 teaspoons sugar

METHOD

Crush the cardamom, cinnamon, peppercorns, and cloves, if using, with a mortar and pestle and set aside.

In a medium pot, heat the water over medium-high heat.

When you see small bubbles at the bottom of the pot, add the tea and the crushed ginger and spices.

When the water comes to a vigorous boil, add the milk. Stir the tea, then let it steep undisturbed with the cover off.

When you see the first rise,* turn the heat off. When the tea sinks to the bottom of the pot, turn the heat back up to medium-high till you see the second rise, then turn the heat off again.

Add the sugar and stir till all of it is dissolved. Strain the tea into a pitcher through a fine-mesh strainer. Aerate the tea by transferring it between the pot and the pitcher a few times or by using an electric frother.

Serve and enjoy!

---

* The "first rise" happens when the contents of the pot slowly rise to the top for the first time. The "second rise" happens almost immediately afterward, when the chai rises to the top for the second time.

How does a vibrant green tea leaf end up as a dark, dry, yet aromatic blend that is completely unrecognizable from its former self?

Most black tea post-pluck processes involve four stages that completely transform the leaf. The first and the most essential step after the leaves are plucked is to dry them on large rotating drums in the tea factory. This withering process is controlled by careful ventilation through fans that evenly distribute heated air through the drums. Drying out the leaves at this early stage ensures that they are malleable enough to be further processed. Depending on the weather conditions, the thickness of the leaf, and the temperature of the air that passes through, the leaves can take anywhere from twelve to twenty hours to release their moisture, which allows for the necessary chemical changes that determine the taste and quality of the tea.

After withering the leaves, workers used to stand on either side of a long table to "roll" the soft leaves in a motion similar to kneading dough. Today, this stage of the drying process is mechanized by using large rollers that rotate in opposite directions with just enough pressure to mimic hand rolling. The heat generated during the rolling process removes more moisture and separates the bud, the first leaf, the second leaf, and other large leaves so that they can be processed by type later. Rolling the tea leaves also breaks down the leaves at a cellular level, allowing enzymes and chemicals that were previously separated by cell walls to interact with each other, releasing the complex flavors of each tea leaf that wouldn't have been evident otherwise.

After the rolling, the leaves are spread out on the floors of well-calibrated fermentation chambers for one to three hours at a time. However, from the moment they are plucked, tea leaves start undergoing a process of oxidation, or fermentation, at the end of which the leaves change from their bright-green hue to a dark copperlike tone. Heat and air levels are carefully monitored by humidifiers and ventilators that keep the moisture level of the chamber between the optimal temperatures of 80°F to 85°F (26°C to 29°C). Interestingly, to this day, the extent of fermentation of each batch is decided by "taking nose"—a manual process undertaken by experienced "nosers" who know when to stop the process and transfer the tea to the next stage through their keen olfactory senses.

The last stage prior to the sorting and grading of the tea is a heating process that arrests the fermentation. Hot air at temperatures ranging from 185°F to 260°F (85°C to 126°C) is blown through the fermenting tea laid out on long conveyor belts. By this stage, the moisture content of the tea leaves is less than 3 percent of its original composition and is further reduced by passing the leaves through another dryer before sending the leaves off to be graded.

This journey of leaf to liquor, of plant to powder, might be comparable to what some psychologists describe as navigating a "liminal space." The word "liminal" comes from the Latin root "limen," which means "threshold"—a limit of capacity, ability, or intensity that, if exceeded, will cause a shift or change in the status quo. Navigating a liminal space, then, could mean existing between places where change is the only constant. I like to think that chai leaves go through a liminal space of sorts when they transform through this four-stage process, experiencing constant flux due to variable factors like heat, moisture, and pressure, and retaining the core qualities for which they were harvested while transforming into a symphony of flavor and aroma.

What's happening during this process—what many describe as the core steps of chai making—is, at some level, akin to what has happened to us on a global scale. COVID-19 put all of us into one big, disorienting liminal space. You and I were in limbo, not fully where we had been, and also not where we were supposed to be. Our former ways of doing and being were altered and contested. Plans changed. Programs changed. People changed. The systems we used to rely on were called into question. Just as billows of heat break down the tea leaves in the drying vessel, the different seasons of the pandemic disoriented our lives at the deepest levels, obscuring our visions of the past, upsetting the opportunities of the present, and clouding the possibilities of our future. Caught between lockdowns and mask mandates, between one travel restriction and the next, you would have experienced what sociologist Corey Keyes calls "languishing"*—a sense of "meh-ness" that feels somewhere between burnout and flourishing. In this state, it's hard to be fully engaged in anything as you experience apathy and indifference. This is a mode of living marked by worrying uncertainties, glimmers of happiness, sharp vulnerabilities, and ambient anxieties.

The Christian monks during the early fifth century also had a word for this. In the first few centuries after the death of Jesus, many of them ventured into the wilderness to spend time in solitude, a practice that Jesus had often done during his ministry. But when these desert "fathers" and "mothers" were away, they often experienced an inability to concentrate, a sense of hopelessness, or feelings of lethargy and purposelessness. The name they gave to this mix of emotions was "acedia," a term borrowed from ancient Greek that meant "lack of care." This took on a more spiritual tone when the monks used it to describe a psychological and spiritual state where one experiences a deep, inner sadness that leaks into every area of one's life.

Whether you call it "languishing" or "acedia," chances are that you have gone through these seasons in the past. Heck, you may even be in one right now. It feels like a silent mourning— your imagination interrupted, your hopes hindered.

---

* Corey L. Keyes, "The Mental Health Continuum: From Languishing to Flourishing in Life," *Journal of Health and Social Behavior* 43, no. 2 (June 2002): 207–22, https://doi.org/10.2307/3090197.

You may be in the wilderness. And it's harsh.

But the wilderness can also be a place where newness can emerge.

Right after my eighteenth birthday, the time between finding out that I couldn't afford tuition for my freshman year at college and the moment when the funds showed up in my account a few months later was, yes, a time of frustration, but also one of clarification. For the first time in my life, I was away from my family in what felt like a wilderness. But it was in this wilderness where I was forced to dig deeper into my faith. This liminal space marked by uncertainty and loneliness pushed me to revisit the beliefs that had been taught to me as a child and to explore anew their relevance in *my* world and *for* the world.

During my sophomore year in September 2011, right before I took a year off from college to teach at the Bouchrieh Adventist School in Beirut, I asked Elynn to be my girlfriend. The space between asking her and the next time we would see each other was a space of disorientation but also of maturation. This liminal space pushed both of us to learn new ways to communicate with each other, propelling us toward new levels of intimacy in our dating relationship. We would enter the wilderness again a few years later when we dated long distance for four more years while we were pursuing our graduate studies. After eight years of knowing each other and learning how to love each other through our ups and downs, on July 9, 2017, in the presence of many witnesses, we both said "I do" to accompanying each other through the many liminal spaces yet to be encountered.

Likewise, the one-and-a-half-year space between when we found we could no longer meet in person at our church because of COVID and when we resumed our services was a space of disruption but also of innovation. The wilderness pressed us to develop our virtual presence through livestreaming, virtual gatherings, and digital solutions to nurture and disciple our members. This liminal space forced us to revisit our liturgy and our core traditions and caused us to reenvision contextually relevant ways to serve our community during unprecedented times.

In these spaces, as we're caught in flux between one safe place and the next, and beneath the shifting and fluctuating layers of anxiety, uncertainty, and vulnerability, we can still find refuge in the core of ourselves.

And ultimately, I think that's what these drying moments in our lives can eventually point us to. If you, like the "nosers" during the fermentation process, can involve your senses and your agency to fully experience these challenging moments instead of trying to avoid or bypass them, the dross might slowly dissipate to eventually reveal:

The bedrock of your beliefs.

The foundation of your feelings.

The trajectory of your desires.

The shape of your loves.

The core of your character.

The essence of your hopes.

The structure of your systems.

And the scaffolding of your soul.

Come to think of it, "chai making" might be an inaccurate description of the four-stage process. You see, this drying process doesn't actually *make* chai; it simply *reveals* what chai is truly made of. The liminal space that chai goes through, from leaf to dust, is not a transformation of chai as much as it's a revelation of it. The withering, rolling, fermenting, and heating affect the leaves to such an extent that their true essence is both released and retained as they transform. The drying doesn't determine chai's nature; it secures it. The drying doesn't create its flavors; it preserves them.

I don't know what liminal spaces you have gone through so far. I don't know how much languishing you've done or how much listlessness you have felt. But whatever your situation, I believe that these difficult, drying times can also be refining, revealing times. During your time in this space, your priorities may narrow, your loves may deepen, your preferences may shift, and your values may sharpen.

A teaspoon of chai looks completely different from the hills where it was harvested. And when it hits the warm water in your pot, the leaves undergo a rebirth. They slowly unfurl, releasing all their flavors that were carefully challenged and preserved during the drying process.

Bestea, when you've walked through your chaos, traversed through the disorienting heat, and eventually crossed over to the other side into your next anchor point, whether you realize it or not—and I hope you do—you are going to be blessed with new flavors.

Flavors that are going to surprise you. Flavors you didn't know you had in you. Flavors so unique, so sublime, so life-giving that they are anything but dry.

CHAPTER 6

recipe

Pursuing Mastery through Love

Kesar (Saffron) Chai

Serves 2

INGREDIENTS

3 green cardamom pods

1 cup filtered water

2 teaspoons loose leaf Assam CTC* black tea

1 cup full-fat milk

2 strands saffron, plus more for garnish (optional)

2 to 3 teaspoons sugar

METHOD

Crush the cardamom with a mortar and pestle and set aside.

In a medium pot, heat the water over medium-high heat.

When you see small bubbles at the bottom of the pot, add the crushed cardamom.

When the water comes to a boil, add the tea.

Stir the tea for 1 minute, then add the milk and saffron. Stir the tea, then let it steep undisturbed with the cover off.

---

* Refers to the "cut, tear, curl" tea processing method.

When you see the first rise (see page 55), turn the heat off, add the sugar, and stir till all of it is dissolved.

Strain the tea into a pitcher through a fine-mesh strainer. Aerate the tea by transferring it between the pot and the pitcher a few times or by using an electric frother.

Garnish the tea with a strand of saffron in each cup if you want a stronger saffron flavor.

Serve and enjoy!

I never measure when I make chai.

Maybe because I've gotten lazy. Maybe because I like to live life on the edge. Or maybe because I've been making my own thethani for the last fifteen years, and after all this time, it's been boiled down (pun intended) to an art.

After adding the water to a pot over medium heat, I wait to see small bubbles forming at the bottom. That's when I know that the water is at an optimal temperature to activate the essential oils of the spices and the ginger. I then add a teaspoon of crushed spices—cardamom, cinnamon, peppercorns, and cloves—and a teaspoon of crushed ginger. When the water starts to boil, I add one and a half to two teaspoons of either Assam or Ceylon loose leaf black tea. In a few moments, the spices and tea will begin their dance, so I close the lid to give them some privacy. After about two minutes, I open the lid and add full-fat milk. Immediately, the party hits a pause, but I keep adding milk until I see the color of the chai liquor turn into the complexion of a Happy Brown Boy™.*

After the milk gets acquainted with the spices and tea, it's only a matter of time until the temperature of the mix rises to the point of almost boiling over the pot. At that moment, I immediately turn the heat off completely and watch the chai settle back into the pot. But as soon as it settles, I crank up the heat to

---

* If you want to be more precise, there's a literal paint color called Chai Tea Latte at Home Depot with its own color code. What a time to be alive.

the highest setting so that the chai can boil again. When the chai reaches the top of the pot the second time, I turn the heat off completely. I stir in a few teaspoons of sugar, strain the chai through my fine-mesh metal strainer into a thin-lipped frothing pitcher, and then aerate it by pouring the golden drink back into the pot and then into the pitcher again. I do this a few times until I see a foamy layer on top of the chai. Finally, I transfer it into two cups: one for my wife, and one for me. I take a sip. All is well in the world.

After more than a decade of making tea for myself and my friends, I've come to appreciate "feel" as an equally, if not more, legitimate method of measurement. அம்மா (Amma)* barely measured. Dada changed up his methods all the time. My பாட்டி (paatti)† never transcribed her recipes. So when I go by "feel" rather than simply following a recipe, I'm reminded of my roots as I attempt to walk in the path of my predecessors' mastery. Whenever I choose to experience the moment rather than striving for accuracy, when I measure with the *heart* rather than with the head, I feel more at home in my practice of making chai.

So, naturally, I never wrote any of my recipes down in the past. But all that changed in January 2020, when I posted an Instagram story of my masala-chai-making process. My DMs were inundated with questions about measurements and methods. During this time, I was experimenting with TikTok, a very

---

* "Mom" in Tamil.

† "Grandmother" in Tamil.

new short-form video application that had gripped the attention of every kid in my youth group. Without overthinking it, I took screenshots of the stories, recorded a voice-over detailing the process in an entirely unhelpful, ridiculous way, slapped everything together into a one-minute vertical video, and uploaded it on TikTok.

Nothing could have prepared me for what happened next.

That video racked up more than three hundred thousand views in less than forty-eight hours. I had to turn my notifications off because I couldn't keep up with the likes or comments that had variations of the following request: "Where is the damn recipe?" Today, after more than three years of creating food content online, transcribing recipes for our "bestea" community of half a million people who are united by their love for chai, and seeing the great lengths to which my food creator friends go to craft perfect recipes, I'm convinced that there's more to this obsession with recipes than I'd previously realized.

The word "recipe" comes from the old Latin root "recipere," which means "to take" or "to receive." In the late fifteenth century, a recipe was simply a formula for a remedy prescribed by a physician. At its core, a recipe used to be a simple set of rules, a method that had been created for the sole purpose of providing for someone in need. It used to be about service. But I believe this "other-orientation" of recipes has changed somewhat over the years.

Today, a recipe has become more of a power text. Transcribers and sharers of recipes are often seen as more influential than, say, an ආච්චි (aachi)[*] who knows how to make the best dal[†] but hasn't written anything down, or the grandfather who makes the best watalapans[‡] but without a recipe. A quick scroll through Instagram will reveal that those who have the best image grid and the clearest recipes are, at first glance, seen as authorities on their crafts even if they don't have cultural roots in them. Opinion pieces by popular chefs are considered legitimate just because they have a blue tick next to their name on social media, even when they critique foods that are not part of their repertoire or cultural background.

So, between a chai fanatic like myself who has written down a few recipes and a chaiwalla[§] from the streets of Kolkata who has no digital footprint, take a wild guess as to who's seen as more influential or important? Days and years of making chai, mastering its art, loving the craft—somehow sidelined by a few viral TikToks. It's an unfortunate reality that in a culture of image management, the clarity of a recipe and the charisma of its writer are often assigned more value than the stories and origins behind the food. The visible is assigned more value than the obscure. And if we go by that metric, I fear that we'll continue to

---

[*] "Grandmother" in Sinhala.

[†] A household lentil dish eaten with rice, roti, or bread.

[‡] A popular coconut custard made with jaggery introduced by the first Malay settlers in Sri Lanka.

[§] A tea seller or vendor in the Indian subcontinent.

miss out on the culturally rich and beautifully complex stories of individuals who haven't *written* anything out but have *lived* it out.

I suspect this obsession with recipes, at least in part, is perpetuated by the subtle myth that having access to the right information will eventually lead to the right formation, that knowledge about a particular area can directly translate into becoming a specialist in that field. But author James K. A. Smith counters this idea by suggesting that perhaps we humans are not just "thinking things"—brains on a stick who develop primarily through information acquisition—but creatures of desire who are shaped not only by what we know but, more importantly, by what we love.* The things we love, and the people we are loved by, shape us more than the things we know.

If that's the case, then attaining true mastery—like the chai-walla in Kerala or my paatti—is not just about expertise or the method with which it is legitimized but also about the exercise of love. It's not just about how much work you put into perfecting your craft but also about how that work is expanding your capacity to serve others with compassion. What if mastery is achieved not simply by putting in ten thousand hours of practice but also by your relationship with each second of those hours? Did you love what you did? Did you love through what you did? Did you enjoy the anticipation of serving through your craft as much as engaging with that process? I believe true mastery in anything—whether

---

* James K. A. Smith, *You Are What You Love: The Spiritual Power of Habit* (Grand Rapids, MI: Brazos Press, 2016).

it be in making chai or writing poetry or creating a new line of code—is a by-product of countless hours of hard work allied with an other-oriented purpose. It transcends the limits of a formula—a recipe—and enters into the realm of relationships.

In precolonial and preindustrial eras, children learned to cook beside their mothers and grandmothers. Ammas and chithis learned to make their flavorful concoctions by helping their paattis. One can even argue that mastery in bygone eras was not so much a thing to be pursued but more a way to live. Family members rarely had the choice of opting out of adopting and perfecting their family's practices and rituals, because they needed to pass them on to the next generation. In this way, a family became a sociocultural nexus embodying their rituals, each member practicing, and in turn being formed by, their craft in such a way that even future generations would be blessed.

That's why I like to think that the chaiwalla, my dada, and my paatti have, in fact, achieved true mastery. It isn't a form of mastery that was achieved by obsessing over perfection or pre-cision. Their excellence was not a result of practicing their craft in a silo. Instead, it was as if they were one with what they were making. Food and drink, their compositions; the kitchen, their conservatory. For them, making chai was not about blindly im-plementing a recipe for its own sake, but about creating a sym-phony of love, directed toward those who were willing to listen. I may have more head knowledge about thethani than Dada, but he certainly has more experiential knowledge about it by loving the process more and loving his children and wife through it. Perhaps the main difference between Dada's tea and mine is not so much in the flavor as it is in the care; he's made more cups out of other-centered love than I have. The time he's spent thinking about the well-being of his family has seeped into his tea making, transforming earthly flavors into something transcendent.

Dada came to visit Elynn and me during the winter of 2019. It was a joy having him with us and, more importantly, making Sri Lankan delicacies for us. Amma was the one who usually cooked for us growing up, but since he was the only one here, he realized that he had to quickly learn how to cook dishes that only she used to make. I wasn't surprised by what he did next.

He didn't Google the recipes. He called Amma.

I'll always cherish the memories of him getting on FaceTime with my mom, even if it meant waking her up at three a.m., to coach him through a dish. Amma didn't seem to mind it either. It was evident that Dada didn't just reach out to her because he wanted help in making a dish; he reached out because he knew that talking to her and making the dish together would create a different experience than just following a recipe from the internet. Deep down, he probably knew that mastering a dish was not just about implementing a sequence of instructions but about accessing a realm of knowledge that could only be unlocked in a loving community.

As I think about my paatti and dada, I can't help but wonder: What could mastery look like today?

What if it looked less like achievement and more like service?

What if it looked less like attaining certain degrees and accolades and more like becoming a certain type of human?

What if it was a way to grow not only wider in your influence but also deeper in your compassion?

What if it looked less like a solo pursuit and more like a communal journey?

What if mastery had less to do with the love of habits and more to do with cultivating habits of love? Like the color of a Happy Brown Boy™ in my chai, these things are hard to measure, but easy to notice over time.

Making chai without a recipe reminds me that sometimes the best things in life cannot be measured.

CHAPTER 7

thirst

Satisfying Needs through Justice

Kenyan Ginger Chai

Serves 2

INGREDIENTS

1 (1-inch) cinnamon stick

4 green cardamom pods

2 cloves

1 cup filtered water

1 teaspoon fresh crushed ginger

2 teaspoons loose leaf Kenyan black tea

1 cup full-fat milk

4 teaspoons sugar

METHOD

Crush the cinnamon, cardamom, and cloves with a mortar and pestle and set aside.

In a medium pot, heat the water over medium-high heat. When the water comes to a boil, turn the heat down to low and add the crushed ginger and spices and the tea. Cover the pot and steep the tea for 4 minutes.

Uncover the pot and add the milk. Turn the heat up to medium-high.

When the tea rises to the top of the pot, turn the heat off.

Add the sugar and stir till all of it is dissolved.

Strain the tea into a pitcher through a fine-mesh strainer. Aerate the tea by transferring it between the pot and the pitcher a few times or by using an electric frother.

Serve and enjoy!

Dada making thethani is my earliest memory of watching tea being made.

Before any of us is up, he starts by placing a pot of water on the stove. While it's coming to a boiling point, he adds full-fat milk powder and sugar into four mugs. He then whisks the contents of the mugs into a thick paste by carefully adding a few drops of the hot water. He turns off the heat after the water reaches a rolling boil. Then he adds a few teaspoons of Ceylon BOPF tea from the estates of Bogawantalawa into the pot of water and allows it to steep for a few minutes. After the kahata* turns a deep brown color, he strains it into the milk paste in the cups, producing the color that inspires the Happy Brown Boy™ hue I aim for in my own chai.

It's magic. Every time.

"That's enough thethani/kiri té for the day," said no Sri Lankan ever. As long as there is room for community, there's always room for tea. Every cup increases the thirst for more. If I have chai today, I must have chai tomorrow. If I make it twice, I'd want to double it tomorrow. It is indeed a beautiful paradox that tea satiates thirst and also creates it, deliciously reminding the drinker that to thirst, at the most primal level, is to be human.

---

* Tea liquor—the tea mixed in with water.

But this thirst for "more" has not always been righteous. A brief look into the history of tea will reveal that a thirst for tea catalyzed the thirst for empire, prolonging the British occupation of South Asia for centuries. In the 1820s and early 1830s, British colonists started growing export-quality tea in India and Sri Lanka primarily in an effort to limit the Chinese monopoly on tea and secure its imperial interests through the East India Company (EIC), the world's most powerful industry at the time. This was a long, drawn-out process that involved much bloodshed and exploitation and continued to feed imperialism, the primary engine of colonization. For about six hundred years prior to the British arrival in Assam, the Ahom people from Burma,[*] a neighboring country whose influence overflowed into India before the colonial period, ruled peacefully until the British found wild tea trees during the Anglo-Burmese War of 1824. The Ahoms did drink tea in their communities, but it wasn't until the colonization of Assam by the British that tea would become more than just an herb consumed during sacred rituals. The trajectory of this thirst-quenching mission, particularly in India, is best encapsulated by Charles Bruce, one of the "discoverers" of the tea shrub in Assam, who in 1836 wrote, "I would like to go back to the Singpho country[†] to make a few presents to those [native leaders] who may be favorably disposed to our objects, I therefore hope the guns and pistols are

---

[*] Myanmar.

[†] Modern-day Assam, India, specifically in the districts of Tinsukia, Sivasagar, Jorhat, and Golaghat.

on their way up, the very sight of which would make them promise anything."[*]

This thirst for more would be reanimated later in the early 1930s when the world economy was spiraling downward. During this time, Great Britain had to find a way to unite a fragile empire and improve its unemployment rates. Part of this collapse involved a crisis in the tea industry, and thus planters and colonists, along with key political figures, came up with the "Drink Empire Tea" campaign, a mass advertising strategy aimed to entice consumers, politicians, and business owners to buy tea in order to protect the empire's reputation in the world. Marketing experts manufactured a thirst for tea by using everyday household objects to depict compelling stories highlighting imperial power over and against its subjects. Pictures of exotic lands and melanated people from South Asia juxtaposed with images of affluent tea-drinking British aristocrats were used to convince the masses that the "East" was but an "annex of Manchester," that to buy "Empire Tea" was to claim their stake in perpetuating Western supremacy.[†] Advertisement became a tool for colonization, rekindling thirsts by rewiring consumer habits.

But when you keep exploiting people's thirsts, it's only a matter of time before it backfires. This is what happened in 1773 when Great Britain passed the Tea Act, which allowed the British-run EIC to sell tea duty-free to the colonies while still

---

[*] Erika Diane Rappaport, *A Thirst for Empire: How Tea Shaped the Modern World* (Princeton, NJ: Princeton University Press, 2017), 101.

[†] Rappaport, *A Thirst for Empire*, 246.

putting pressure on the American colonists to pay heavy taxes to the British. On December 16, 1773, a group of American separatists who called themselves the "Sons of Liberty" came onboard three EIC ships docked in the Boston harbor and emptied out more than ninety thousand pounds of tea, which would have a monetary value of nearly a million dollars today, into the sea. This bold act of rebellion against the British Empire would fan the flames of the American Revolution and eventually form the United States of America.

History reveals to us that while all thirsts are human, not all thirsts are moral. My thirst for a cup of chai is qualitatively different from a thirst for empire. A "bad" thirst, when satisfied, may benefit one at the expense of others. In contrast, a "good" thirst is a pursuit of a good that, when quenched, will lead to the flourishing of yourself and the people around you. Good thirst, like "good trouble,"* is often triggered by a need that is felt by many and that, when satiated, will not only satisfy the one thirsting but also enrich the lives of countless others. If we allow it, good thirst can even index our energies toward the work of reforming unjust systems and resuscitating marginalized communities. This is what happened, for instance, in January 1940 during a strike by under-

---

* A famous battle cry of late civil rights leader and Georgia congressman John Lewis: "Get in good trouble, necessary trouble, and help redeem the soul of America."

paid Tamil plantation workers on the Mooloya Estate in Hewa-
heta, Sri Lanka. After one of their kin, a laborer named Govindan,
was shot dead by a police officer for protesting the refusal to pay
one of his colleagues, their persistent thirst for just wages and fair
opportunities was mobilized into collective action when all the
laborers in the hill country resigned en masse from the plantations. The colonists had no choice but to acquiesce to their request, the first of a series of actions that would catalyze Sri
Lanka's independence from British rule on February 4, 1948.[*]
Seventy-five years later, at least one thing is clear: Our thirsts are
here to stay. We have seen the bad thirsts of corrupt politicians
satisfying their own interests at the expense of the people. Sri
Lankans, in particular, have seen the good thirsts of the අරගලය
(aragalaya)[†] where the proletariat took to the streets to protest
unjust and oppressive systems of power. Tapping into our collective memory as a defiant and courageous nation transformed our
thirsts into a force to be reckoned with.

I believe chai can beckon us to taste not just the flavors of the
current moment but also the thousands of moments that preceded
it. So with every sip, we enter into a history of resilience, purpose,
and hope that existed even before our awareness of tea. As the
sweet drink slowly becomes a part of us, we're reminded that there
were others who thirsted before us, whose thirsts sparked move-
ments, liberated thousands, and created opportunities for change.

---

[*] Richard Simon and Dominic Sansoni, *Ceylon Tea: The Trade That Made a Nation*
(Colombo, Sri Lanka: Colombo Tea Traders' Association, 2017), 146.

[†] "The revolution" in Sinhala.

Bestea, we may not be able to quench our thirsts permanently, but perhaps we can learn how to thirst *well*. To thirst well means to be aware that our thirsts make us more, and not less, human. To thirst well is to believe that your legacy is not limited by, and to, your current experiences.

I long for the day when I get to have thethani again with Dada. In the meantime, as I perfect my own recipes for chai and for my life, being keenly aware of the many desires that will pull me in many directions, I'm going to try to live a life characterized by generosity rather than greed, shaped by an abundant mindset rather than a scarcity mindset, and indexed toward justice rather than apathy.

How about you?

CHAPTER 8

crush

Maturing through Pain

Indian Masala Chai

Serves 2

INGREDIENTS

3 green cardamom pods

1 (1-inch) cinnamon stick

4 fennel seeds

2 peppercorns

1 clove

1 cup filtered water[*]

1 teaspoon fresh crushed ginger

2 teaspoons loose leaf Assam CTC black tea

1 cup full-fat milk

3 tablespoons sugar

METHOD

In a medium saucepan over medium heat, lightly toast the cardamom, cinnamon, fennel, peppercorns, and clove for 15 seconds. Crush the toasted spices with a mortar and pestle and set aside.

---

* In many parts of India, chaiwallas omit the water and just use milk as the base. If you want to try a milk-only version of this recipe, just add the spices and tea to 2 cups of whole milk instead.

In a medium pot, heat the water over medium heat. When you see small bubbles at the bottom of the pot, add the toasted spices and the ginger.

When the water comes to a boil, add the tea. Stir for 1 minute.

Add the milk. Stir the tea for 1 minute, then let it steep undisturbed till the tea rises.

When you see the first rise (see page 55), turn the heat off. When the tea sinks to the bottom of the pot, turn the heat back up to medium-high till you see the second rise, then turn the heat off again. Stir in the sugar till all of it is dissolved.

Strain the tea into a pitcher through a fine-mesh strainer. Aerate the tea by transferring it between the pot and the pitcher a few times or by using an electric frother.

Serve and enjoy!

n August 2021, I went backpacking for the first time in my life with a group from my local church. It was a 6.1-mile trek with an elevation gain of around two thousand feet from the Fernandez trailhead located in the Sierra National Forest in northeastern California. During the first thirty minutes of the hike, I felt like I was on top of the world—soaking up the smog-less, unvarnished beauty of the wilderness and chatting up a storm with my youth group and their parents. But the voices got progressively quieter as we kept moving up the hill.

Within an hour into our ascent, I knew this trip was a mistake.

Every step was difficult. Every breath, labored. My back was now damp with sweat from prolonged contact with my Kelty backpack, which was supposed to make my life easier. It didn't, or maybe it did; I couldn't think straight anymore. I started to go through a mini quarter-life crisis as I observed how I, a thirty-one-year-old, was struggling to keep up with some of the parents of my youths who were years older than me. *Is this the beginning of the end?* I thought as my body unconsciously drifted toward the back of the line.

Stumbling toward a distant summit, unsure of the destination but forcing myself to take the next steps, reminds me of the journey my ancestors might have taken a few centuries ago. Between 1860 and 1947, over three million people were separated from their families and sent on a one-way trip to work the tea plantations in Sri Lanka, and my great-great-thaatha from my dad's side was very likely among that number. Like them, he would have been a "coolie"—a loan word from South Asia meaning "servant" that was picked up by Portuguese colonists as early as the sixteenth century and then used by the British to differentiate indentured servants from the rest of the population. In the early nineteenth century, the British were the first to experiment with the coolie trade at the tail end of the African slave trade that was being outlawed with the Slave Trade Act of 1807. With the loss of free labor to power the many industries throughout their colonies, the British brought Indian and Chinese low-wage laborers to fill this vacuum on their sugar and cotton plantations and railway constructions on a more contractual basis. While proponents of indentured servitude viewed it as "ethical labor," historians claim that this coolie trade was a way for European colonists to enjoy the benefits of slave labor while creating the illusion of free labor.[*] As a 1950 publication on tea described, "The coolie trade of Assam was reminiscent of the slave trade conducted between Africa, America, and the West Indies."[†]

But the bitter aftertaste of injustice and marginalization is still experienced by plantation workers to this day. A recent study investigating the health of tea laborers in northeastern India shows

---

[*] Lisa Lowe, *The Intimacies of Four Continents* (Durham, NC: Duke University Press, 2015), 196.

[†] "Tea Promotion in West Africa," *Tea Promotion* 3 (May 1950): 2–5, quoted in Rappoport, *A Thirst for Empire*.

that despite the Plantations Labour Act of 1951,[*] years of unfair wages, inadequate healthcare, and restricted education, especially for women, have continued to endanger their well-being.[†] After the decolonization of Sri Lanka in 1948, up-country plantation Tamils—the cultural heritage of my parents—have continued to be the most underprivileged and marginalized ethnic minority group on the island because of state-sanctioned violence against them from successive post-independence, nationalistic regimes.[‡] This began soon after the Ceylon Citizenship Act No. 18 of 1948[§] was enacted, by which nearly one million plantation Tamils, roughly 11 percent of the Sri Lankan population at the time, became stateless and were denied privileges reserved only for the Sinhalese majority.

To add insult to injury, in 1956, right after Ceylon independence from colonial rule, then president S. W. R. D. Bandaranaike won a landslide victory in the general elections for promising to enforce the Sinhala Only Act, which would effectively replace English with Sinhala as the only official language of a new Sri

---

[*] This act is an official government agreement to ensure the welfare of labor and regulate the conditions of work in the tea plantations of an independent India.

[†] Preety R. Rajbangshi and Devaki Nambiar, "'Who Will Stand Up for Us?' The Social Determinants of Health of Women Tea Plantation Workers in India," *International Journal for Equity in Health* 19, no. 29 (2020), https://doi.org/10.1186/s12939-020-1147-3.

[‡] International Movement against All Forms of Discrimination and Racism, *Racial Discrimination in Sri Lanka* (UN Committee on the Elimination of Racial Discrimination, July 2016), https://imadr.org/wordpress/wp-content/uploads/2016/07/IMADR_Sri-Lanka_CERD90_July2016.pdf.

[§] This act states that anyone who wishes to be granted citizenship in Sri Lanka needs official documentation to prove that their parents were born within the new borders.

Lanka. This was done to the exclusion of the Tamil language, which was spoken by almost a third of the country,[*] resulting in the oppression of Tamils and the eventual demand for a separate Tamil nation-state, Tamil Eelam, leading to the Sri Lankan civil war that lasted decades. Although the war ended in 2009, prejudice against Tamils, particularly toward Tamil plantation workers, is still alive and well. My ancestors toiled through the British occupation, fought for their emancipation, and persisted against the systemic marginalization of Tamils that continues to this day in my home country.

Despite the odds, or perhaps *because* of them, these individuals transformed and repurposed their struggles into focused action. For instance, did you know that the act of adding crushed spices to chai—like in a masala chai—originated from an act of protest? Before World War I, chaiwallas began to add masala to tea, which, up to that point, tasted very bitter. In response, the Indian Tea Association, mostly made up of British tea estate owners, sought to prevent the spread of this practice because they thought that less tea would be used per serving with the addition of these spices. Tea stalls that used masala in their chai were shut down and replaced by those that didn't. But this did not stop the explosion of the growth of masala chai, as Indians saw it as a tastier version of tea—and also as a way of reclaiming their history by making chai their own.

Adding lightly crushed spices to their tea was a protest

---

[*] Indian Tamils, Sri Lankan Tamils, and the Moors.

against injustice, a practice that symbolized their quest toward eventual independence from colonial rule. That's why, to me, a cup of chai is a cup of courage. A cup of thethani is a cup of perseverance. Chai memorializes in taste the legacy of those who alchemized their pain into purpose, their misery into meaning, and their suffering into salvation. And that's why I'm proud to be a descendant of a coolie. I'm proud to be part of a lineage of courage and determination.

The more I connect with where I came from, the clearer I get about where I'm heading. The more I connect with this history, the more it reframes my day-to-day life. When the protests against anti-blackness and systemic racism were happening in the United States, I found reference points from my own story to help me navigate questions surrounding racism and privilege in this nation. When the farmers' protest was happening in India, I was able to empathize by looking at what some of my family members might have gone through in the tea plantations. The crushing periods of my personal history continue to provide moral context to help me understand the complex periods of our collective history. I think if my great-great-thaatha could see me now, doing what I'm doing and living the life I'm living, he'd probably be shocked. Though he was denied a better future for himself in many ways, he faithfully worked the plantations knowing that at least he had the ability to ensure his descendants would have one.

Five hours later, I stepped onto flat terrain. After climbing uphill for an hour, this felt like a gift from God. At this point, almost everyone was ahead of me, and I wondered if this was the last leg before we would hit our base camp. A few minutes later, the forest cleared out on my left, revealing one of the most beautiful sights I'd ever seen.

It was an alpine lake that looked like someone had Photoshopped a high-resolution picture onto nature. The water was as clear as glass, perfectly reflecting the mountains; there were two skies in my view—one above me and one on the water surface. I dropped my backpack, went to the water's edge, and took a deep breath. The air was crisp and sweet. I kept staring at this place in disbelief as I felt the exhaustion slowly exiting from every pore of my being.

In the thick of this experience, I had been too focused on the struggle to realize that facing the difficulty of the mountain before me enlarged the capacities within me. Every step exposed my limits, but taking the next step expanded them. German American theologian Paul Tillich wrote that suffering introduces you to yourself and reminds you that you're not the person you thought you were. It carves through the floor of what you thought was the basement of your soul and it reveals a cavity. Suffering messes up your usual routine of life and almost forces you to recognize that there's more to you than you thought existed.

Maybe this is why tea estate laborers are some of the toughest people I know. Years of suffering and injustice have opened up their beings and fired up their souls. The well-coordinated worker strikes and intentional actions for better futures in many estates reveal that they are still able to sow seeds of hope, which, more often than not, tend to flourish in the soil of adversity.

Every sip of chai, then, if you will allow it, can invite you to take a deeper look, not only at the complex history of what's in your cup but also at the difficulties in your own life. If you look closely, I believe that beneath the pain, the cruelty, and the violence to our soul is a foundation of moral joy, an incandescent posture of being that radiates from an inner core, strengthened by struggle and fortified by a commitment to justice.

The next time you reach out for the mortar and pestle to prepare the spices for your masala chai, I invite you to pause. When were the "crush" periods in your life? When was the last time you felt deep pain and suffering?

Maybe it was the loss of a loved one. Maybe it was the end of a relationship. Maybe it was the termination of a job. Maybe it was a silent battle within yourself.

Maybe it is seeing the injustice, oppression, and chaos in this terrible, beautiful world we live in.

My friend, as you see the spices transform before your eyes, as you sense their different aromas merging into a singular aura, may I remind you that as long as you choose to take one more step forward, these moments are expanding your capacity to love, your ability to feel, and your courage to act. These moments have the power to transform your story into a saga, as you face what comes to you boldly and bravely. These moments can be the stuff that legacy is made of, as you now get to pour into others from the reservoirs of your own history.

May you find, in the midst of your loss, a lake of love. May you find, in the midst of your tears, a wellspring of healing. May you find, in the midst of your pain, a palace of clarity.

So keep climbing, bestea. And when you're at the mountain-top, after crossing the threshold of your suffering with others who care about you, may you rest in the knowledge that even if you were to descend one day into another tough experience, you're going there confident that there's more in you, and more to you, than you previously realized.

CHAPTER 9

cup

Structuring a Meaningful Life

Tandoori (Kulhad) Chai

Serves 2

INGREDIENTS

3 green cardamom pods

½ cup filtered water

1 teaspoon fresh crushed ginger

2 teaspoons loose leaf Assam CTC black tea

1½ cups full-fat milk

3 teaspoons sugar

HARDWARE

Two small unglazed clay cups (kulhads)[*]

METHOD

Crush the cardamom with a mortar and pestle and set aside.

In a medium pot, heat the water over medium heat.

---

[*] You can get these on Etsy or online specialty shops that make clayware in bulk.

When you see small bubbles at the bottom of the pot, add the crushed cardamom and ginger.

Meanwhile, heat the clay cups over an open flame until they become almost red hot. Keep rotating the kulhads over the flame with tongs so that they're heated evenly.

When the water comes to a boil, add the tea and stir for 1 minute.

Add the milk. Stir the tea for 1 minute, then let it steep undisturbed till the tea rises to the top of the pot. Turn the heat off.

Stir in the sugar till all of it is dissolved. Strain the tea into a pitcher through a fine-mesh strainer.

Place one hot clay cup inside a wide-based metal container (e.g., a metal bowl or a deep metal tray) and pour the chai into the cup. The chai will overflow into the container because of the heat in the clay cup. Pour the overflow chai into the other clay cup.

Serve and enjoy!

magine savoring your chai.

You're done drinking it. You look at your cup, then lift it up in the air . . .

. . . and smash it on the floor.

This is a sight you'll see in parts of India and Pakistan where chaiwallas sell kulhad chai—a masala chai served in small, handle-less clay cups that are typically unglazed and unpainted. Archaeologists say that kulhads have been present in the Indus Valley Civilisation for more than five thousand years, making their use one of the longest-standing ancient traditions continuing to the present day. Kulhads are made in the same kilns used to make other earthenware, but unlike clay pots used to cook meals, kulhads are meant to be single-use and disposable. This makes drinking from them more hygienic, and, since they are biodegradable, they are certainly more eco-friendly than plastic cups.

The dimensions of a kulhad are important. Typically, they can range between 2.2 and 2.8 inches (5.6 and 7.1 cm) in diameter and can hold 5½ to 6 ounces (160 to 180 ml) of chai. The smaller quantities of chai make it affordable to most people regardless of their income level or class status, allowing everyone from all walks of life to be refreshed by a few sips of garam* chai in the midst of their busy schedules. The size of the cup also ensures that the flavors are just right—not too muted or too strong.

---

* "Hot," as in of a high temperature, in Hindi.

I am convinced that chaiwallas on the Indian subcontinent, including the tea makers in Sri Lanka's many kopi kadés,* are magicians. They have mastered the art of extracting just the right amounts of spice, texture, and body from large quantities of tea into each cup, where the dimensions of a single cup determine the direction of their process. While it takes skill to prepare a cup's worth of ingredients for each serving of chai, it takes some sort of wizardry to prepare ingredients for large batches and still be able to present each cup with a perfect blend. Even after making large batches of chai for groups over the years, I'm not sure if I've nailed down the ideal flavor profile per cup yet. While the ingredients give chai its flavor, and the brewing methods its texture, the cup used for chai holds its experience. The height, length, and depth of the cup, while limiting the quantity of chai, preserves its quality at a particular moment. The vessel provides a real-world, finite boundary to house an intangible encounter that lingers in your senses long after your last sip.

We live in an age of hyperindividualism where many believe that the best life is an unbounded life; that the righteous life is an unrestrained life, or that the purposeful life is a prodigal life. But just as you can't have good chai without the right cup, you can't have a good life without the right constraints. Navigating the

* "Coffee shop" in Sinhala.

various complexities of our day-to-day lives requires creating life-operating systems and structures that may feel restricting and inconvenient at first but are essential in orienting us toward a meaningful existence.

I chose my life-operating system when I was a sophomore in college. My dad was a nominal Catholic and my mom was a Hindu before they met in college and chose to orient their lives according to the Way of Jesus in the Seventh-day Adventist (SDA) faith tradition. I was born into a family of committed Adventists. We did all the Adventist things like attending church, keeping the Sabbath, and avoiding alcohol and "unclean" foods.* Even though I had many friends who did not share my religious beliefs, or who lived in countries where Christianity was a minority religion, I felt at home in my faith.

But that would change when I became a sophomore in college.

I had never been interested in being a pastor, but the people at my home church kept encouraging me to pursue it because I had been a decent communicator at a young age and crushed every Bible Bowl in my youth.† When I moved to the United States, I applied to the theology program at Andrews University—the flagship institution of the SDA Church—and got accepted. My

---

* Seventh-day Adventists believe that the Bible promotes a healthy, well-balanced diet as a key to spiritual, emotional, and physical wellness. To that end, as a denomination, they continue to uphold the distinctions made in Leviticus 11 about which type of foods to consume or avoid.

† It's like *Jeopardy!*, but for super-Christians. Fun fact: I went to an all-boys Catholic school during my middle school years in Sri Lanka and made the cut for the Tamil Bible Bowl team. We ranked second all-island that year. Thank you very much.

first year went well, but it was only a matter of time before the doubts about faith and questions regarding Adventism that I'd suppressed eventually burst out into a raging torrent, not dissimilar to how a chai pot overflows and creates a mess when left unchecked. My mind was a mess. But I didn't reach out to anyone about these questions. I couldn't afford to, because as a new immigrant to the United States, my need for survival outweighed my need for clarity. I'd become a "culture chameleon," preoccupied with constantly changing my external behaviors to blend in with my surroundings, not realizing that my internal belief systems were breaking down. My faith began to unravel. I began entertaining the thought that maybe Christianity was a "house of cards," where one issue, if left unresolved, would eventually invalidate and destroy the entire structure. I was also disheartened by how prominent institutions within my religious tradition kept "majoring" in the "minors," making them increasingly irrelevant in a world where they zealously answered questions no one seemed to be asking. I eventually came to a point where I found myself going to my religion classes in order to learn about a God I no longer believed in.

Fast-forward a few months.

I shared my heart with my college best friends, Ashok and Jordan. I told them that I didn't know if I believed in God anymore. I was expecting them to be shocked or disappointed, but instead, in that moment, they chose compassion over condemnation, acceptance over apologetics, and empathy over exegesis. To this day, I don't think they realize how much of an impact they had on me during that time in my life. Through the nonchalant, simple, noncoercive witness of their lives, they made me wonder if sometimes the best ministry happens when it's not done for the purpose of "ministry."

Inspired by their unconditional care in the ensuing weeks, I was forced to revisit my Christianity. *If this is working for them and other people I love, why is it not working for me?* I wondered. I went back to the Scriptures. I reached out to my professors with my questions. I studied. I read. After finding sufficient evidence to be confident in the resurrection accounts of Jesus Christ of Nazareth, I eventually became convinced that the Way of Jesus, as a life-operating system for being human, was historically verifiable, philosophically coherent, cosmologically hopeful, spiritually holistic, emotionally healthy, relationally just, and aggressively other-oriented. But while this persuaded my mind, it didn't affect my heart.

The heart change came soon after.

As I was relearning and revisiting everything about my belief system, or my "cup," memories of my father during my younger years gripped my subconscious and would not let me go. After an exhausting day of studying, adapting, and surviving, my last thoughts before I knocked out for the night were usually about home. I remembered how I used to wake up in my room in Oman, put on my high school uniform that Dada had neatly ironed and kept crisp an hour prior at five a.m., and walked out to the living room to have my breakfast. On my way to the table, I'd see Dada kneeling down on the couch, praying for Khayali, my mother, and me every morning with a Bible opened to a portion of the Psalms. What I had thought was regular and commonplace back then—the quiet, consistent spirituality of a Sri Lankan Tamil man inspired by an undying love for God and family—eventually became a "boat" of memories that helped me navigate the choppy seas of doubt and discomfort, straight into the loving embrace of God.

I woke up from this same dream of memories on a regular Monday. Typically, I'd ignore it, get ready for class, and rush out the door. But that day I sat on my bed in the Meier Hall men's dormitory and closed my eyes. I talked to Jesus. I usually started by saying "Our gracious God" or some other invocation that felt anything but honest, but today I wanted to try something new:

"அண்ணா . . ." ("Annah . . ."),* I began.

I wanted to say more, but I knew I didn't have to. That became the whole prayer. Because, for the first time in my life, captured by the love of my friends and the faithfulness of my father, I chose to see myself not as a slave of a capricious deity or a pawn of religious institutions but a sinna thambi—"little brother"—of a compassionate Older Brother.

It's been more than a decade since then. The Way of Jesus has been, and continues to be, my "cup." But it may not be yours. Maybe it used to be, but others forced you to drink from it in a way that caused you to shelve it forever. Maybe you smashed the cup into smithereens after it was used as a tool of manipulation in your life rather than a vessel for liberation. Maybe you have a

---

* "Elder brother" in Tamil. (Can also refer to a male cousin.)

different cup. Maybe your cup isn't even a cup, but some type of vessel to hold . . . something. Perhaps you know the dimensions of your cup, but you're in the process of clarifying its definitions. At any rate, I encourage you to take some time to think about your cup today.

How do you define "freedom"?

Where do you draw your boundaries?

What are your spiritual, physical, emotional, professional, or relational limits?

What constraints could give your life an added sense of meaning and purpose?

What are the qualities you'd like to have in a life-operating system?

The cup that holds my chai reminds me that limits may not be the enemy of a meaningful life but a vehicle for creating one. In environments where convenience is glorified and freedoms are idolized, I believe that value-driven, well-thought-out, and intentional restrictions on the self can create "fences" that can help us cultivate a flourishing garden of life.

Bestea, as you drink from your cup, feel its form. Think about your constraints. I pray that the limits you've chosen will guard your being.

May the structure of your life continue to give shape to your gently unfolding story.

heat

Stewarding Our Attention

Pakistani Doodh Patti Chai

Serves 2

INGREDIENTS

3 green cardamom pods

1 cup full-fat evaporated milk

1 cup full-fat milk

1½ teaspoons loose leaf BOPF black tea

4 teaspoons sugar

METHOD

Crush the cardamom with a mortar and pestle and set aside.

In a medium pot over medium-high heat, combine the evaporated milk, full-fat milk, and crushed cardamom. Keep stirring so that the milk doesn't stick to the bottom of the pot.

When you see small bubbles on the surface of the milk, add the tea. Keep stirring.

Aerate the tea by using a ladle to scoop up the tea and release it back into the pot.

Once the tea turns a light brown shade, turn the heat off and stir in the sugar till all of it is dissolved.

If you want a deeper color, you can heat the tea for longer before adding the sugar, but periodically lift the pot a few inches from the flame so that the tea doesn't overflow.

Strain the tea into a pitcher through a fine-mesh strainer. Aerate the tea by transferring it between the pot and the pitcher a few times or by using an electric frother.

Serve and enjoy!

was fourteen years old when I got arrested.

It was the summer of 2014 in Nawalapitiya, Sri Lanka. I was at the home of my பெரியம்மா (periyamma)* on our annual family trip from Oman, where we'd immigrated two years prior. After dinner, she handed a document to me and said:

"Intha ingilish enakku velanguthilla, thambi. Konjam paathuttu sariya irukkanu sollureengala?" ("I can't understand this high English, Kevin. Can you check it and let me know if everything is okay?")

This was supposed to be an official visa approval document from the German embassy in Sri Lanka that her son—my cousin—had obtained recently. He had apparently gotten accepted by an employment agency that contracts laborers from Sri Lanka to work in Germany. I was oblivious to many things as a middle schooler. But after seeing how my parents had struggled with their visa paperwork to get to Oman—the countless days spent ensuring that all the information was accurate—I already knew that something was off about this document.

I really wanted to go play outside. But I forced myself to be in the moment, to pay attention to the document in front me to help my annah and periyamma.

At first glance, there were way too many typos for it to be an official document. It was supposedly a German visa, but there wasn't

---

* "Mom's older sister" in Tamil.

a single line of German. The preparer's credentials also sounded inauthentic. I expressed my suspicions to my periyamma and told her that I would stop at the German embassy when our family was going to be in Colombo—the capital city—the following week.

A week later, I was standing at the gate of the German embassy with my சித்தப்பா (sithappa),* whom Dada had sent to go with me. I handed over the document to the security guard and explained everything. He took it inside. After what seemed like an eternity, a white Jeep approached us from the other side of the gate, and two men walked out.

One of them flashed his ID, which said "CID" in bold letters. They were cops from the Criminal Investigation Department, members of one of the most feared branches of police in Sri Lanka.

"Are you the ones who brought the fraudulent documents?" he asked rudely in Sinhala.

I was right! I thought, feeling something between relief and anxiety for what was about to happen next.

"Yes, sir. I got this from—"

"Come with us immediately," the man said as he pointed to the back seat of the Jeep.

I pressed in closer to my uncle as my heartbeat and thoughts raced at a million miles per hour. *Am I going to jail? What are they going to do to us? Will I see my family again? I should have been nicer to Khayali!*

My fear quickly turned into anger.

---

* "Dad's brother" in Tamil.

Where is my cousin? He should be here instead of me! I should have never offered to do something like this. My grip around my uncle's wrist tightened by the second. However, I soon realized that getting mad without careful thought and action was not going to make anything better. I directed the frustrations I was feeling into intentional attention. I started to go over the possible scenarios that my uncle and I could end up in and began to silently plan for different outcomes.

Eventually, we got to the CID headquarters in Pettah, in northwest Colombo. The cops ushered my uncle and me to the elevator, and we went to the highest floor, which, I later found out, was where the most notorious cases were deliberated on. They seated us in front of the deputy inspector, who had a stern but clean-shaven face; he then motioned for them to leave.

"How did you get these papers?" the deputy inspector asked us.

I took a look at my surroundings.

Inhale.

Exhale.

"Sir," I began in my "whitewashed" Sinhala, possibly interrupting my sithappa and surprising the inspector by going first. "I have no idea who's responsible for this. My aunt showed this to me and said that her son had paid a large sum of money to a travel agent who'd promised to grant him an employment visa to Germany. The document did not look legitimate, so we took it to the German embassy to see if it was valid."

The inspector furrowed his brow. I started praying that I would have a nice cellmate.

He inspected the document. Then looked up at us.

"All right. Looks like you have nothing to do with this. This seems to be another hit in a fraud case we've been working on. Just wanted to check if you both were involved. We'll look into this. You're free to go."

I couldn't believe my ears. Without a moment's delay, the same men who had taken us in ushered us out of the building. They returned the documents, and we called out for a tuk-tuk[*] and somehow were on our way home.

Paying attention not only saved us from possible imprisonment but also got justice for my periyamma and annah. Choosing to be present, to permit yourself to experience the moment in its entirety, opens more space for you to entertain more perspectives than your own. And when that happens, it allows you to not just take care of your own needs but also bring awareness to the needs of others.

Paying attention to the heat is probably one of the most crucial steps in the chai-making process. You can have the best ingredients, the best equipment, and the ideal recipe, but ultimately the quality of your chai will depend on your heat management.

Here are a few points in your chai-making process when you should pay more attention to your heat: If you plan on toasting the

---

[*] A three-wheeled vehicle commonly used as a taxi all over the island.

spices prior to crushing them, you only need ten to fifteen seconds in a pan over medium heat to get a bold, smoky chai flavor. It's important to toast whole spices rather than pre-crushed or powdered spices because the higher surface area of powdered spices can cause them to burn faster and will make your chai unpalatable.

If your chai requires a 1:1 ratio of water to milk, add the crushed spices along with your tea to simmering water (185°F to 205°F/85°C to 95°C), and when the water comes to a vigorous boil, immediately add cold milk to arrest the heating process. Overboiling the water can remove oxygen and hydrogen molecules from the water when it converts into steam, which makes the tea taste flat. I also add the spices to simmering water because boiling the spices in water for more than a minute can overextract the oils from bold spices like cardamom and cloves, making the chai chalky and bitter. The same can happen to the tea—black teas like Ceylon BOPF and Kenyan BOP release tannins that produce the astringency required to balance out the thickness of the milk, but when oversteeped, these teas can release more tannins, resulting in a bitter tea.

For chais with a milk-only base, like doodh patti, I add the tea and spices to the heating milk roughly thirty seconds after I've turned on the heat. I keep the heat constant on a medium-high setting throughout the process, stirring the chai for a few minutes only at the beginning. Constant stirring of the chai also affects the process because the agitation increases the time it takes for the tea to rise to the top of the pot, which is when I know the chai is ready.* It's also important to note that different types of milk have different boiling points. While it's not entirely necessary to memorize them, it is helpful to note the variety lest you overheat some and underheat others.

The more present you become to the process, paying close attention to visual cues and smells, the better your chai is going to be.

The quality of your chai depends on the quality of your attention.

In this case, what's true for chai is true for life today: The quality of our lives depends on where and how we direct our attention. In a world of information overload, there are countless demands for our attention. The primary capital traded between entities is information—data that can generate sales, drive revenue, and cause systemic change. It's no surprise, then, that the more control a corporation has over the information that is being traded every second, the more power it has over shaping societies.

This information costs us our attention. Your attention and mine. In an age when we live much of our lives online, navigating reality through little rectangles in our hands, the effective-

---

* Unless I let it do a "second rise," a technique explained in more detail on page 132.

ness of digital media is determined by its ability to retain human attention.

So we need to be mindful of where we're directing our attention. Singaporean writer Tan Hwee Hwee, who became burned out in New York from juggling her corporate job with her book writing, reflects on the relationship between attention, beauty, and the formation of the self. After finishing the second draft of a manuscript and sending it to her editor, she booked a trip to Italy. While in Rome, upon reflecting on the past few years of her life, she penned the following:

> *Beauty is anything—an object, words on a page, the sound of music—that stills the soul and fills it with joy, peace, and love. . . . As I looked at those objects in Italy, the more beauty I saw, the more beautiful I felt inside. I began to understand a profound but simple truth: you become what you contemplate.*

She noticed that what you pay attention to affects not only how you perceive the world but also who you are. If you keep placing beauty in front of your mind's eye, you become beautiful. If you keep placing disturbing content in front of you, you tend to become anxious. What you focus on doesn't affect just your outputs but also your outlooks. The latest developments in brain research also show that what we pay attention to physically

---

* Tan Hwee Hwee, "In Search of the Lotus Land," *Quarterly Literary Review Singapore* 1, no. 1 (October 2001), http://www.qlrs.com/issues/oct2001/essays/lotusland.html.

organizes and reorganizes our brain maps.[*] Perhaps the oft-repeated saying "Repetition deepens the impression" is true, even at a physiological level.

When I make chai, it becomes a feast of attention: a pure, immersive celebration of a moment that, like Rabbi Abraham Heschel's description of the Sabbath, is a "palace in time."[†] The more I stay in that sacred moment, tinged with notes of cardamom and jaggery, the more I realize that mindfulness and beauty are friends, and that they usually travel together on the pathway paved by intentional attention.

But our overdependence on digital media to alleviate our anxieties has short-circuited our abilities to be present to ourselves and to the world around us. That's why I believe that making chai, or engaging in any meaningful ritual without the internet at your fingertips, is a protest against the attention economy. Every time I embrace "boredom"—a choice to explore the possibilities of a single moment without relying on the appendage that is my phone to escape from it—I realize how often I see every second as a resource to be commodified rather than as a gift to be received. I realize how often I sacrifice the beauties of the "now" to satisfy the urgencies of the "next." In an age of unprecedented access to information and, with it,

---

[*] Sara Bernard, "Neuroplasticity: Learning Physically Changes the Brain," Edutopia, December 1, 2010, https://www.edutopia.org/neuroscience-brain-based-learning-neuroplasticity.

[†] Abraham Joshua Heschel, *The Sabbath: Its Meaning for Modern Man* (New York: Farrar, Straus and Giroux, 1951), 15.

tools of distraction, maybe choosing to be "bored" is choosing to taste the fullness of a moment. Reframing boredom as fully "attending" to the present, as an encounter with your deepest self, rather than as an evil to be exorcised, allows you to befriend reality.

But this is hard work. Being alone with your thoughts, even for a moment, may be one of the most courageous things you can do for yourself. Whether you're in a meditative mode, out in nature without your AirPods, or just sitting in your living room with your chai but without your phone, it's only a matter of time until the thoughts that you've suppressed or the memories that you thought you'd forgotten gently rise from the recesses of your being to the brim of your mind. In that moment you have a choice: Are you going to choose to distract yourself because you are afraid of interacting with them? Or are you going to meet them where they are?

I want to remind you, bestea, that in the midst of that overwhelming moment of fear, your response will mean the difference between possible growth and staying where you are. The fear you feel when you face your inner self is your body's motion sensor telling you that you're about to step into an arena that's going to stretch you beyond your imagination. The fear you feel in solitude is not what you fight, but *where* you fight. That fear is not the thing that prevents you from growing; it's the *place* of your growing. So when you choose to meet the moment, instead of escaping from it, you allow yourself the possibility to rise from where you are to where you could be:

from confusion to clarity,

from hurt to hope,

from despair to determination.

Your awareness becomes the seed of impact that grows in the soil of your world, as you recapture the wonder that is in and around you to grow into a forest of possibility, change, and reformation.

So once you've mastered a few recipes and don't need to reference a TikTok or a recipe on a screen, the next time you make chai, leave your phone in another room. Resist the pull to multitask by turning off that podcast episode. Save it for your next drive. I hope you have your tools ready. Feel the coolness of the mortar in your hand. Smell the symphony of the spices as you open your masala dabba.* Let yourself be surprised by the sizzle of the water hitting the heated pot. Bask in the sweet and savory vapor emanating from your brew. Watch as the foam dances its way to the top. Turn the heat off. Feel the soft heat under your towel as you carefully lift the pot and strain the chai into your pitcher. Let yourself wonder about the stories behind the spices that you see on top of the mesh that are being bathed in the milky river. Time to aerate. Embrace the reality that you might spill some chai; no worries. Give yourself the courage to fail, even if it's just for this one moment. Allow the steam to caress your face as your pour the foamy, velvety liquid gold into your cup. See? There's more than enough for you. And maybe for someone else as well.

---

* A steel spice container used in the Indian subcontinent that can store up to seven spices.

And as you cup the effervescent elixir, may the gentle heat against your palms remind you that you are alive.

You are present.

You are right where you need to be.

You are attending now.

You are becoming beautiful.

CHAPTER 11

boil

Embracing the Process

Kashmiri Chai (Pink Chai)

Serves 2

INGREDIENTS

½ cup room-temperature filtered water

3 tablespoons Kashmiri tea leaves[*]

5 green cardamom pods

2 cloves

1 (1-inch) cinnamon stick

¼ teaspoon baking soda, plus more if needed

½ cup ice-cold filtered water

1 cup full-fat milk

½ cup half-and-half

Pinch of salt

3 tablespoons sugar, plus more to taste

1 tablespoon raw sliced unsalted almonds

1 tablespoon raw sliced unsalted pistachios

---

[*] I like to use the Tapal brand Kashmiri chai, but if you can't find it, you can also use nonbitter loose leaf green tea leaves.

METHOD

In a medium pot, combine the room-temperature water, tea leaves, cardamom, cloves, and cinnamon. Heat the mixture over high heat.

When the mixture comes to a boil, add the baking soda. Aerate the tea by using a ladle to scoop up the tea and release it back into the pot for 6 to 7 minutes. This mixture will reduce down and turn a deep pink color. If it doesn't turn pink, add another ¼ teaspoon baking soda.

After the color turns a deep pink, add the ice-cold water. Keep aerating the tea with your ladle for 1 minute, then add the milk and half-and-half.

When the tea comes back to a boil, turn the heat off.

Add the salt and sugar and stir till all of it is dissolved. Keep adding sugar till you get the desired sweetness.

Strain the tea into a pitcher through a fine-mesh strainer. Aerate the tea by transferring it between the pot and the pitcher a few times or by using an electric frother. Pour the chai into cups, then add the sliced nuts to garnish.

Serve and enjoy!

W hen I make chai, there are five stages in my boiling process.

Making the perfect cup of masala chai requires adding different ingredients at each of these stages. After making a cup almost every day for the last decade, I've started to look for the following visual cues that let me know what stage I'm in.

A few minutes after turning the heat to medium-high, I see small bubbles that look like little eyes lining the bottom of the pot. This is when I usually add the spices so that the water will become a flavor canvas for the chai.

As the temperature rises, the small bubbles start to wiggle their way to the top of the pot and join larger ones to form bubbles that look like squid eyes. During this stage, I typically add my loose leaf black tea.

In the third stage of the boiling process, the tea is at or almost at the boiling point of 212°F (100°C). I see bubbles joining other bubbles on their way to the water surface, creating a long stream resembling the soapy bubbles that kids blow on a summer day. When I see this, I immediately add full-fat milk to the pot.

I call the fourth stage of the process the "first rise." At a certain temperature right before the boiling point, the light-brown brew that was quietly rolling and bubbling breaks out into a vertical wave and rushes its way to the top of the pot. It happens so fast. I wait until the violent foam reaches almost to the top, and then I turn off the heat completely. Apart from the aeration process, this is where I've messed up the most. If you're not especially attentive during this stage, you're likely to drink "stovetop"-flavored chai.

I call the fifth and final stage the "second rise." This is an optional stage in the chai-making process, but I have found it to deepen the flavors of some chais and bring out their creaminess even more. After I've turned off the heat, I wait for a few seconds. When the foamy chai eases back into the pot, I crank up the heat to the highest setting, which causes the chai to rise again. This happens faster than the first rise since the temperature is already at the boiling point. And just as with the first rise, I turn the heat off when the chai almost reaches the top. Then I add my sweetener of choice.*

I know what you're thinking. "But, Kevin, can't I just put everything in all at once and boil it until it's ready? I don't have the energy or the time for five stages!" If that's you, I don't blame you. Although this entire journey takes seven to ten minutes for two cups of chai, I, too, find myself looking for ways to save time. But making homemade chai, embracing its process, and reflecting on my life experiences have made me realize that in most cases, the *efficient* way to do something may not always be the most *effective* way to do it.

---

* If you don't see these rises, it's because (a) the base of your pot is too broad, (b) you have too little chai liquid in your pot, or (c) you're using a nonfat milk that doesn't rise as well as full-fat alternatives.

I wish I'd known this thirteen years ago when I came to the United States as an eighteen-year-old with two suitcases, a backpack, and a few Benjamins. Prior to that, I had been living in Oman with my family. All of us had applied for the Diversity Visa Program through the U.S. government, which granted permanent residencies to eligible applicants once they'd been cleared through U.S. Citizenship and Immigration Services. The cleared applications were then entered into a lottery system where, if you were chosen, you would qualify for an interview at the U.S. embassy in your country. Out of the four of us who applied, I was the only one who qualified for the visa interview. Within a span of a few weeks, I had gone from being unsure about my post–high school life to getting on a plane to the United States.

Why me? I kept asking while I struggled to sleep during my first few months in White Oak, Maryland.

Why couldn't Amma, Dada, and Khayali come?

Why did my relationship of four years in high school end right before I left the country?

Why didn't anybody tell me that these separations were going to hurt this much?

Even as a third culture kid (TCK)—someone who has spent significant portions of their early life in different parts of the globe—this move was excruciatingly difficult. I knew that for my parents, saying goodbye to their son on October 27, 2008, at Bandaranaike International Airport in Colombo was probably one of the hardest things they ever had to do, so for the longest time I didn't open up about my disorientation and fear. As their firstborn and a first-generation immigrant, I told myself that the best gift I could offer my family, in return for all they had done, was to be my own independent success. In my pursuit of significance, I sacrificed closeness with them at the altar of achievement. I knew I had to keep going, even if I had to do it on my own. Even if it meant that I wouldn't let them know what was really going on.

Adaptation became survival. I did everything I could to blend into the circles I was a part of, even if it came at the cost of my comfort. In a desperate attempt to belong, I owned the identity that was given to me by my friends at my youth group—FOB (fresh off the boat), exchanging my self-esteem for communal acceptance. My accent became my armor. My humor, my sword. I wore my peculiarity as a crown, seeking to legitimize my presence in the places I was in, not realizing that deep down I was still a fearful Sri Lankan boy, seeking approval as validation for my existence.

But I realize now what I hadn't noticed then: The heat had always been on in my life.

little eyes . . . squid eyes . . . soapy bubbles . . .

I eventually started college. I found community—teachers and mentors—who, by teaching me how to think, helped me reframe my life story. I fell in love again. Elynn and I started dating, and after five years, we graduated together. I was offered a sponsorship to pursue higher education. After three years, I was the first person in my family with a master's degree.

. . . first rise . . .

I got married to Elynn and started a new life in San Diego as a student pastor. I moved from a basement to an apartment, minutes away from the Pacific Coast. We adopted two fur children, our cats Phoebe and Leo. I had the highest privilege of journeying with high school and college students, helping them to identify their purpose and calling. I became part of a church community that loved and accepted us. I found contentment.

... *second rise* ...

And upon reflecting on the last decade, I realize this:

What I had seen as *wasted* heat was simply *stored* heat. What I had seen as heating without change was simply a second rise waiting to happen. What I had perceived as a mundane life, without noticeable progress over weeks and months, was simply a life that was about to burst into a joyous existence in a few years.

And when it happened, it happened fast. It felt like a breakthrough.

And breakthroughs take time. King David of Israel was anointed at age seventeen, but he wouldn't be crowned until twenty years later. Abraham Lincoln was elected into the state legislature in 1830, but it took him more than thirty years of enduring defeat after defeat to finally be elected as president. Jesus was called at birth to fulfill a specific mission, but he wouldn't start his ministry until age thirty. He ministered for three years in relative obscurity with his disciples, after which the Jesus movement spread across the globe in thirty years and continues on to this day.

We tend to think that change is linear and sequential, like a smooth, uniform incline. We are tempted to think that the path to success is incremental and predictably progressive. But when it doesn't necessarily look or feel like change is happening, energy is simply being stored for a momentous shift. As long as the heat is on, the rolling boil will happen. It's not a matter of *if* but *when*.

I don't know what you're hoping for. I don't know what you've prayed for. Regardless of what it is, the time between your prayer request and the fulfillment of a promise is the exact amount of time needed to prepare you for the promise. This is a crucial time when your flavors are deepened, perspectives are broadened, and visions are widened, so that you can not only handle the promise when you receive it, but you can also gift it to others as it continues to steep into your story.

So reframe the wait. Embrace the process. Because who you are becoming through the process is often more important than what you're getting out of the process. May you realize that efficient ways of being will not always produce effective ways of loving. I hope you know, sooner or later, that it's hard to love when you're rushing. May you recognize that every detour, every curve ball, and every frustration that you've gone through has catalyzed the ongoing process of your becoming.

The heat has been on.

But hold on, bestea. You're not wasting. You're simply steeping.

And that breakthrough?

It is coming.

CHAPTER 12

wait

Resting as a Revolutionary Posture

Vanilla Chai

Serves 2

INGREDIENTS

4 green cardamom pods

1 (1-inch) cinnamon stick

½ cup filtered water

1 teaspoon fresh crushed ginger

2 teaspoons loose leaf Assam CTC black tea

1½ cups full-fat milk

3 tablespoons sweetened condensed milk

1 teaspoon vanilla extract

METHOD

Crush the cardamom and cinnamon with a mortar and pestle and set aside.

In a medium pot, heat the water over medium-high heat. When you see small bubbles at the bottom of the pot, add the crushed spices and ginger.

Right before the water comes to a full boil, add the tea. Stir for 1 minute, then add the full-fat milk.

Aerate the tea by using a ladle to scoop up the tea and release it back into the pot. When the tea rises to the top of the pot, turn the heat off.

Stir in the sweetened condensed milk and vanilla extract. Strain the tea into a pitcher through a fine-mesh strainer. Aerate the tea by transferring it between the pot and the pitcher a few times or by using an electric frother.

Serve and enjoy!

I hated the Sabbath.

And it didn't help that I was born into Adventism, a Christian denomination that observes a weekly Sabbath from sunset on Friday to sunset on Saturday. This practice is rooted in the first few pages of the Bible, where God rests for twenty-four hours after creating the world. Later, when God gives the Torah to Moses to govern a new republic, God commands them to "remember the Sabbath day, to keep it holy,"* lest they forget the slavery and the dehumanization they'd endured in Egypt. The Sabbath, therefore, is a weekly reminder that humans have intrinsic worth because they were created by God, and thus are liberated from the pressure to ultimately prove themselves through their work.

But it became clear to me, even at a young age, that keeping the Sabbath day "holy" meant different things to different Adventists. It seemed that for our family, and for many other South Asian Adventists, the Sabbath was mainly about the things we couldn't do rather than the things we could. I couldn't watch my favorite cartoons. I couldn't play my video games. I couldn't sing or hum secular songs. I remember feeling embarrassed when I had to tell my friends that I couldn't hang out with them on Friday nights or Saturday mornings because I had "church." Khayali and I had something to do at church almost every week, and

---

* Exodus 20:8 (English Standard Version).

I recall feeling rushed by my parents on weekends so that we wouldn't be late to the service.

But all that changed when I came to the States as an immigrant.

Being alone for the first time in eighteen years in a foreign country caused me to revisit the practices that had made me. In the absence of my family, I heard the murmurs of my heart. Silence felt like violence as I was forced to confront desires that I never knew existed. I longed for home. I longed for community. I longed for purpose. Out of sheer desperation to connect with my roots, I started to keep the Sabbath.

For a Sri Lankan freshman in college, the Sabbath became a soul detox, a weekly booster shot to inoculate me against the disease of hurry that I saw around me. Time, in Sri Lanka and Oman, felt slow and leisurely; for the most part, people recognized that there was more to their lives than the work they did. But during college in the States, I'd slowly absorbed the lie that my value was dependent on my performance. I thought I wasn't doing enough because everyone around me was rushing to get stuff done while I was struggling to keep up. So I revisited the Sabbath. It was only a matter of time before the practices that had once felt like a killjoy—being away from social media, fasting from pop culture, turning off the news, leaving homework for Sunday—helped me realize the benefits of restraint and the meaningfulness of rest. I was less exhausted, functioning more from a place of fulfillment rather than from the fumes.

My attitude toward the Sabbath also shifted when I focused less on the limits of the practice and more on the new freedoms that were just now becoming visible to me, although they had always been there. I spent my Sabbaths investing in a local youth group. I shared a meal with friends unmediated by screens. I reconnected with my family in Oman. I visited other South Asian community members in my college to enjoy homemade chai and carrom.*

One meaning of "Sabbath" in Hebrew is simply "to stop." To cease from your work and to choose rest. The ancient prophets realized that it's often when you pause that your purpose on earth slowly begins to reveal itself. To me, this weekly twenty-four-hour practice reinforced the belief that my ultimate life trajectory was perhaps not toward professional validation but toward existential rest. I rested on the Sabbath, and the Sabbath rested me.

I realized I didn't have to rush.

I was free to only be. To rest. To offer rest.

To me, chai is the Sabbath in a cup. Moments of rest, punctuated throughout the chai-making process, can be gentle reminders of the waiting that must be embraced lest you rush past your natural pace. You have to wait for the ginger to flavor the water. You have to wait for the tea to boil. You have to wait for the milk to change color and froth up toward the top of the pot. You have to

---

* A popular tabletop game commonly found in South Asian homes.

wait for the boil to subside. You have to wait for the chai to be strained. You have to wait for the chai to be aerated. You have to wait for the chai to be poured into the cup. You have to wait for the chai to cool down.

Waiting, in this sense, is not about impatience to reach future possibilities but about an expectant remaining in the moment so you don't miss out on the gift of the present. To wait for your chai is to rest in anticipation.

But resting does not mean inactivity. Resting does not mean being passive or disengaged. Rest is not the opposite of work but the fulfillment of it. To rest is to be at home with the realization that the work you have been doing is meaningful to you and its beneficiaries. Resting is different from taking a break; the latter involves catching a breath amid the stresses of your work, while the former involves appreciating that you are worth more than your work.

Sometimes when I rest during my chai-making process, I remember that my parents didn't know how to rest either. Not because they didn't want to, but because they couldn't afford to. They labored, tirelessly attending to their patients' needs day after day, and oriented their entire lives around the needs of Khayali and me, often sacrificing their own in the process. The only times that I remember them truly resting was when they slept at night—I can still hear my mom's snores—which, I reckon, were sweet because they were earned.

While my parents' work ethic has inspired my own, I wonder if perhaps this is why I have a rather dysfunctional relationship with leisure. I feel anxious when I take breaks. I feel guilty for not working on something all the time. I feel shame, slowly radiating from within, at even the thought of not capitalizing on moments between responsibilities. Whenever I go on vacation, I struggle to rest because of the knowledge that a good portion of my family in Sri Lanka may not have access to the privileges that I have. The story I tell myself is that I need to at least pretend that I'm busy all the time so that they don't think that I'm lazy, unsuccessful, or ungrateful.

That's why I wonder if the prevalence of toxic productivity and hustle culture, especially among immigrants in general and South Asian immigrants in particular, is at least partially due to us seeing profession as devotion and work as worship. Whether they are religious or not, most South Asians seem to attribute a sort of divinity to their parents, viewing them as saints— exemplars and forerunners of the good life that they, too, would like to enjoy one day. And unable to emancipate themselves from family expectations, some of them begin to view career success as a form of tithing, an offering of gratitude toward their loved ones to exemplify a life well-lived. It becomes difficult to do work for work's sake, to engage in one's vocation for the pleasure of it rather than for its use. When this happens, approval is glorified and fame is lionized, while self-care is marginalized and boundaries are stigmatized.

But waiting when making chai reminds me that there is more to my humanity than my hustle. While waiting for my thethani to almost boil over, I wonder if the struggles that my parents went through to create a bright future for us is somehow cheapened, even invalidated, when I see my successes as appeasements. They didn't break their backs so that their son could break his while trying to win their approval. They worked because they loved me. They hustled because that's what love does. So probably the best thing I can do, in gratitude for what they have done, is to see success as a lifestyle of unconditional love and ample opportunities to rest, instead of as a stepladder toward upward mobility.

Resting, like gratitude, is a revolutionary act in an age of ambient anxiety, a brave posture that asserts the value of your humanity amid attention- and energy-exploiting industries that seek to harness your best energies to fuel their own capitalistic ends. Choosing to rest is choosing to resist systems that require our resilience. Just because we *can* be resilient doesn't mean we always *have* to be. In this hyperconnected, finger-swipe age where convenience is idolized and inconvenience is demonized, resting means rising above the "white noise" created by cultural expectations, hidden trauma, and societal pressure, and reclaiming agency over our own soundtrack. Just like waiting transforms raw ingredients into incredible flavors, resting transforms and prepares us to embrace what's coming next. It's in the rest that we grasp the true weight of a moment—its intensity, its density, its possibility.

As a recovering perfectionist and workaholic, I'm trying a few ways to incorporate rest into the rhythms of my life. For one, I take a month-long Sabbath from social media every year to give my creativity a much-needed break. I've felt creative burnout when the pace of my production exceeds the pace of my life. Pausing creation for a month has been therapeutic, clarifying, and rejuvenating. Every week, I try to observe a Sabbath from Friday night to Saturday night. During this twenty-four-hour period, I do engaging and disengaging practices that help me rest. Disengaging practices are those that inspire release: fasting from social media, fasting from the news cycle, and taking a hard break from work-related email and consuming information for my videos. Engaging practices, on the other hand, are those that inspire participation: making chai for friends, sharing a meal with family unmediated by screens, going on a walk outside, and reading a few chapters from a book that I've been putting off because of my busy schedule. When it comes to daily resting, I've been trying to schedule an hour per day just for myself. I don't always succeed at this, but when it happens, it's a time when I do what's best for Kevin Wilson. What do I want to do in that moment to be rested, independent of the views of my wife, parents, or family? Choosing to show up for myself during this time not only brings rest but also reminds me that I don't have to sacrifice my comfort at the altar of others' expectations. I can do things for me. And that is perfectly all right.

So when you make your next cup, bestea, I pray you realize that what's happened *in* you during your resting is more important than what happens *through* you when you work. Your work is elevated because you've had a chance to regroup through rest.

Your rest can help you reframe work as your unique and beautiful contribution to the ongoing adventure of collective humanity rather than as the ruthless exchange of money for your time.

May you believe that busyness and burnout are not badges of honor.

May you realize that hurrying may not only reduce tomorrow's worries but also rob today of its bliss.

May you see rest not as an escape from life but as the realization of its beauty.

CHAPTER 13

Developing Depth through Disorientation

Teh Tarik
(Malaysian Pulled Tea)

Serves 2

INGREDIENTS

1 cup filtered water

½ cup full-fat evaporated milk

1½ teaspoons loose leaf Ceylon BOPF black tea

3 to 4 tablespoons sweetened condensed milk

METHOD

In a medium pot over medium-high heat, combine the water and evaporated milk.

When you see small bubbles on the surface of the milk, stir in the tea and keep aerating it by using a ladle to scoop up the tea and release it back into the pot. You may have to lift the pot a few inches above the flame during this process so that the tea doesn't overflow.

When the chai turns a light brown shade, turn the heat off.

Pour 3 tablespoons sweetened condensed milk into a pitcher. Strain the tea through a fine-mesh strainer into the sweetened condensed milk. Stir vigorously till all of the condensed milk dissolves in the tea.

Aerate the chai by transferring it between the pot and the pitcher a few times, till you see a thick foam appear on the surface of the tea. If the foam is thin, add 1 more tablespoon condensed milk and keep aerating.

Serve and enjoy!

One of my fondest memories of growing up in Sri Lanka was watching the tea masters "pulling" tea at their roadside kopi kadés. After the tea was strained through a fine cloth strainer into a pitcher, the tea masters would pour the contents of the pitcher into another vessel, often making this into performance art. Depending on their mood, they would either stand in one spot while pouring the chai from a pitcher held in one hand above their head into another pitcher held at the waist, or they would spin around while doing this, impressively rotating the pitchers around their bodies without spilling a single drop of chai. I'm salivating just thinking about the sweet, foamy chai they'd pour into a tiny glass cup, offering a moment of bliss to the customer during their busy workday.

I rarely drink chai without aerating it. I do this by first pouring the liquid from my pot into my metal pitcher and then from the pitcher back into the pot, back and forth, four or five times. When you aerate chai this way, the infusion of air molecules not only cools the chai but also makes the drink more "full-bodied" and creamy. If I'm entertaining guests who already know that they are about to get chai, this is the point at which they start recording on their phones. With a towel, I take the steaming pot with my right hand and move it a few inches in front of my face at eye level. I take the pitcher with my left hand and keep it a few inches in front of me by my waist. I take in a breath to focus, and then I pour the foamy chai from the pot into my pitcher. I'm not looking at anyone else, but I hear oohs and ahhs as they, too, are hypnotized by the misty, sweet, golden waterfall that seems to appear out of nowhere. I pray that nothing spills out as I carefully transfer the contents of the pitcher into little cups for my guests. Displacing the chai back and forth transforms a spiced milk tea into a symphony of flavors—effervescent, all its notes activated by a beautiful disorientation.

In my life, this state of disorientation is all too familiar. The constant moving from one place to the next and the repeated trauma of saying goodbye to loved ones cause third culture kids like me to question the stability of their identities. I lived in four countries before age nineteen, and every displacement and transition forced me to change who I was to fit the social and relational contexts I became a part of. When you constantly adapt to ever-changing situations and life circumstances, at some point you can't help but wonder if you are the person you think you are, or if you're nothing but a fraud—an impostor trying to meet the expectations of others.

Battling massive impostor syndrome during this book-writing process has made me realize how much I've struggled with this my entire life. Never in a million years would I have believed you if you had told me that I was going to write a book in my thirties, let alone a book about chai! I was shocked and bewildered when my agent told me that TarcherPerigee was on board to publish my book. But like an ominous fog slowly covering up a beautiful San Diego sunrise, this excitement was soon polluted by an impostor syndrome that slowly crept up within me:

Who am I to write a book on chai? Aren't there people who are more qualified to talk about this? We don't even call it "chai" in Sri Lanka! What will my fellow Sri Lankans think? What will many of my fellow Adventists think about an Adventist pastor writing a book on chai? Should I be staying in my lane, writing a theological or religious book instead? Won't they think I'm "watering down" the Gospel with this book? Is chai really going to be my whole personality?[*]

Our cultural backgrounds can contribute to impostor syndrome as well. Pressure to do well in school, comparisons to others in our communities, or approval that comes from meeting social expectations can cause a lot of people, especially us South Asians, to feel a sense of out-of-placeness later on in life, when we can't outperform someone else in our social or professional circles. When I realized I didn't behave like most of my peers in college, especially those who were celebrated and affirmed by my teachers, I instinctively started trying to outperform everyone else. I created, produced, and performed at high levels, even if it meant sacrificing my identity and sanity in the process. I exchanged who I was for who I thought others wanted me to be.

And it worked.

I started college as "Kevin Wilson, the foreign kid with a funny accent," but by the time I graduated, I was "Kevin Wilson, the golden boy of Andrews University." It wasn't until after I'd gradu-

---

[*] This is probably true at this point.

ated and started working as a pastor and going to therapy that I realized that my productivity was fueled in large part not by my abilities but by my insecurities.

Creation was a coping mechanism. Making was medication. Performance was prescription.

The perfectionism that is first introduced in childhood metastasizes into a culturally accepted disease in our adult lives; we are infected by the belief that we are what we do, that if we do less than someone else, we are somehow worth less than them. This is also exacerbated in honor-shame cultures where social expectations undergird self-worth. "Avunga enna nenappanga?" ("But what will they think?") I can still hear these words from some of my extended family members in my head whenever I'm about to take a path that may be best for me but won't necessarily be understood by them. After years of living according to others' expectations of me, I've come to realize that an important part of being a millennial South Asian, especially here in the West, is practicing the lifelong habit of reclaiming agency. We grow up internalizing the narrative that we are supposed to be who "they" think we ought to be. The older, "wiser," and more successful "they" are, the more power they have over me. But who is Kevin Wilson independent of others' opinions? Who is Kevin Wilson at his core? Who are you at your deepest level?

I wonder if the inability to recognize our inherent value is why many of us sometimes struggle to receive compliments. When was the last time someone congratulated you, and you genuinely believed them? In Christian circles, people often in-stinctively toss out a "praise God" to appear humble when someone celebrates their accomplishments. I can't speak for others, but I've said this not because I genuinely wanted to thank God but because I didn't think I deserved the praise. The story I told myself was that this was simply my duty and not a job well done. I didn't realize that my perfectionism, social ex-pectations, and internalized shame caused me to believe the lie that I had to work *toward* acceptance instead of working *from* it. I believed the lie that I had to work *toward* fulfillment in-stead of working *from* it. I now realize that false humility is as detrimental to the soul as deep pride. They are two sides of the same coin. The latter is an obsession with the self that is driven by self-interest, while the former is an obsession with the self that is driven by shame. The latter is caused by an inability to consider others, while the former is caused by an inability to love oneself. The latter causes a reluctance to give grace to oth-ers, while the former causes a reluctance to receive grace for yourself.

But the delicious foam on the surface of my cup reminds me that the displacements and disorientations in my life need not disorient my identity. The more I move from one place to another, the more I need to reframe my discomfort as a precursor to growth, and my disorientation as a precursor to stability. The more I accept where I'm at, the more I'm able to translate that inner voice of "I don't belong here" to "I am feeling uncomfort-able, and that means I'm growing."

When you aerate your chai—when you "pull" the tea from one container to the other—you may spill some of it. At that point, the voice of perfectionism will whisper to you to stop doing it because any imperfection is anathema. The voice will softly, but sternly, lead you to believe that any display of flaws is unacceptable, and nothing less than perfection is desired of you.

Not true, bestea.

While the need to do "perfect" work may come from good intentions and good rules, perfectionism is a result of being too rigid about those rules.* Perfectionism lets your rules govern your life, rather than allowing your life to teach you more about your rules. For instance, if a rule I have for myself is to do excellent work, then perfectionism will force me to believe that regardless of what season of life I'm in, I have to do excellent work all the time because that's a rule that has helped me in the past. But a healthier perspective would be to take a look at my current season, reevaluate my time and priorities, and then decide what I want to be excellent at and what I'm okay with being "okay" at. That's why I like to think that the opposite of perfectionism is not laziness but kindness. The opposite of perfectionism is being kind to yourself about the rules you have for yourself.

---

* Dan Shipper, Clarissa Ong, and Michael Twohig, "Perfectionism: Why and How to Beat It," Every Media, May 28, 2022, https://every.to/superorganizers/perfectionism-why-and-how-to-beat-it.

So the next time you make your chai, try aerating it.

When you separate the vessels in your hands, right before you pour the chai from one container to the next, I hope you will recall the times in your life when you felt displaced.

When you see the golden waterfall appearing in front of you, the steam slowly embracing your face, I hope you realize that there are more depths to your identity and flavors to your story that are yet to be explored.

As the first sip of that foamy, creamy goodness hits your taste buds, may you realize that when you pulled the chai in different directions, you did not dull its flavors.

You deepened them.

CHAPTER 14

pour

Serving Others with Compassion

Chocolate Chai

Serves 2

INGREDIENTS

½ cup filtered water

1½ cups full-fat milk

2 tablespoons Nutella or semisweet chocolate chips

1 teaspoon loose leaf Ceylon BOPF black tea

⅛ teaspoon salt

4 teaspoons sugar

METHOD

In a medium pot, heat the water, milk, and Nutella or chocolate chips over medium-high heat.

When you see small bubbles at the edges of the liquid, add the tea. Keep stirring so that the milk doesn't stick to the bottom of the pot.

When the tea rises to the top of the pot, turn the heat off.

Add the salt and sugar and stir till all of it is dissolved. Strain the tea into a pitcher through a fine-mesh strainer. Aerate the tea by transferring it between the pot and the pitcher a few times or by using an electric frother.

Serve and enjoy!

climb the mountain near my paatti's house. I'm not alone. In front of me, walking in a line on a path one person wide, are people who look like giants. Their steps are deliberate, and their pace is measured. They are on a mission, carrying lumber, bags of cement, and tools that are bigger than me.

We are on our way to build my periyamma's new house.

I was excited that they were willing to tolerate a ten-year-old in their ශ්‍රමදානය (shramadanaya in Sinhala; siramadhanam in Tamil)[*]—a collaborative service project meant to enhance the lived experience of a person, family, or organization. This practice dates back to 1958, when Dr. A. T. Ariyaratne, a Sri Lankan schoolteacher, took a group of forty students and fifteen high school teachers to a rural village to serve those who were considered untouchables and outcasts by the villagers. Their main goal was to improve their homes, roads, toilets, and schools in order to elevate their quality of life with no strings attached. Shramadanaya's success created a nationwide movement based on the philosophy of Buddhism, the principles of Indian abolitionist Mohandas Gandhi, and ecumenical spirituality.

Local shramadanayas are a microcosm of how Sri Lankans have historically dealt with crises in our country. For instance, the reconstruction of our southeastern coastline after the devastating tsunami of 2004 was, in large part, due to an islandwide

---

[*] "Gift of labor."

shramadanaya effort involving the sacrificial outpouring of time and energy of thousands. It didn't matter if you were Buddhist, Hindu, or Muslim. It didn't matter if you spoke Sinhala or Tamil or just English. When someone talked about doing a siramadhanam, it meant that we were going to roll up our sleeves and get to work. We were one people working toward the common goal of making someone's life a little better than it was yesterday.

I still vividly remember our tea breaks during the shramadana to build my periyamma's house. It was not unusual to have someone designated as the "tea person" whose primary job was to ensure that the kettle was boiling and there was a constant supply of plain tea. Tea breaks punctuated the long phases of work and highlighted our shared feelings of accomplishment during our chats. As we ate our malu banis[*] while sipping on plain tea, I listened to the adults sharing family stories. I observed friends who hadn't seen each other in a long time catching up on their lives and the latest gossip. I saw Dada and my periyappa[†] cracking silly jokes and laughing with my periyamma, tea cups in their hands, sweat on their brows, foreheads glistening in the Nawalapitiya noon sun, completely lost in the joy of meaningful work. The tea that was poured into our cups was emblematic of the meaning that was poured into our hearts. In the heat of service, tea became a symbol for our capacity to pour ourselves out in love for others.

---

[*] A savory bread stuffed with curried tinned salmon.

[†] "Uncle" in Tamil; my periyamma's husband.

In many parts of the world, particularly in South Asia, chai is an elixir of hospitality. At the break of dawn, laborers wait patiently in line on the boulevard close to the famous Red Fort in New Delhi, India, for a van carrying garam chai. It is operated by Sikhs from Sis Ganj Gurudwara, their place of congregational worship just down the road. A Sikh man gets out of the van and pours chai into small glass cups, performing his act of sewa.* What they serve becomes their link to humanity and to their Creator. During that New Delhi dawn, chai becomes an instrument of compassionate service.

That's why when you visit a South Asian, African, Iranian, or Afghan house as a guest, it's very unlikely that you'll leave without drinking a cup of chai. In these cultures, where hospitality is a way to dignify both the giver and the receiver, tea is a potion of honor. Failure to serve your guest is a failure to honor your own family, so the kettle keeps working and the chai keeps flowing. The tea is usually served with some biscuits, cake rusk, or other snacks on the side, which adds more texture to an already beautiful experience. In this way, chai creates a shared space in that living room where host and guest can exchange stories without fear of judgment or condemnation.

I pour my chai three times in my chai-making process. The

---

* Sewa is a foundational practice in Sikhism based on the belief that service with no strings attached is beneficial not only for social relations but also for personal spiritual growth.

first pour happens right at the end after I turn off the heat. I add my sugar, stir, and pour the mixture through a fine-mesh metal strainer into my pitcher. The second pour occurs when I aerate the chai by displacing the liquid from the pitcher to the pot to make it thick and creamy. How many times I do this depends on whether I'm rushing in the morning to get to work, how distracted I am by the beautiful foam, or how much spillage occurs between pours. The last pour happens when I transfer the foamy, aerated goodness into the cups to be served.

Authentic service, like the steps involved in pouring chai, is not a result of a onetime emotional impulse. In order to truly show compassion, provide without reservation, or genuinely be there for someone in need, one must first go through a series of life-changing, paradigm-shifting events where one realizes that others, like oneself, are not invulnerable to the trials and tribulations that come their way. Who comes to your mind when you think of someone who has served you unconditionally? Who gave without any strings attached? Who was there for you when no one else seemed to be? I reckon that the indelible impression they left in your life and the sincerity of their service were less of a knee-jerk, sympathetic response to your need and more of an intentional outflow of a life forged in the fires of affliction.

They knew how it felt to need.

They knew how it felt to want.

They knew how it felt to struggle, sweat, and suffer to the point that they could not help but be activated at their deepest core to serve at the first sight of pain. But the impulse behind this service did not start and end in that moment; instead, their compassion started way back when they first felt their own pain and encountered their own struggles. Service, then, is just the culmination of a lifelong process that has history and context.

As I poured my chai this morning, observing the solids that were left behind in the strainer as the golden liquid seeped into the pitcher, I realized that the first step of the pouring process involves a form of purification. You cannot drink or serve chai without filtering it first.* If not, at best, the solids will ruin the textural experience of chai, or, at worst, the grounds will continue to steep in the chai, making it more astringent and eventually undrinkable. It's no surprise, then, how according to many worldviews, service is seen as a way to purify the self. Regardless of what you believe, I'm sure you've experienced how whole-hearted service has simultaneously enriched the ones you've served while clarifying what makes you "you."

This lucidity was what I experienced during my time as a student missionary in Bouchrieh, Lebanon. I was a sophomore pursuing a bachelor's degree in Christian theology at the time, and I decided to take a year off to serve as a Bible teacher in a K–12 school. I had no prior teaching experience. I had taken zero classes on classroom management. All I had was a curiosity to learn, a thick Sri Lankan accent, and an openness to serve in a new country.

Little did I know that it would be one of the hardest periods of

---

* Unless you are my friend Don, who insists that chewing tea grounds while drinking chai adds to the experience. Big yikes.

my life. During my first few weeks, I had to convince many of my students that I was, in fact, their new Bible teacher and not a new janitor!* The perpetual low-grade prejudice aside, the language barriers between me, the students, and the staff impeded my efforts to build rapport and trust in the community. I had an insane workload because I was the only Bible teacher for the entire school, and I had to come up with the entire curriculum on my own every week. After long days of work, I would drag myself up the metal ladder onto the roof of the dormitory I was staying in, overwhelmed to the point of throwing up and cussing out my angry prayers to a God who I thought had abandoned me.

An African proverb adequately sums up my experience in Lebanon: "A fish knows the beauty of water once it's outside of it." I realize that when I am displaced from familiar contexts, when I choose to put someone else's needs before mine even for a moment, it can often feel like an out-of-body experience that becomes highly clarifying. I didn't notice this while I served. I didn't sense the deepening of my capacities during my time in Lebanon. But I knew everything had changed about me, including feeling a sense of possibility of how much more *could* change in me, once I returned to my "water."

The pandemic has not only taken us out of our water but seems

---

* Many Sri Lankans go to Lebanon and other Arab countries in the Gulf as migrant workers because it allows them to escape corruption and provide a living wage to their families back home, even if it means separating from them for years at a time. This is why Amma left Sri Lanka when I was around four and Khayali was two. Amma would visit us once a year for three months until I was twelve, before we moved together to Oman as a family.

to have thrown the water away during its course. As we were forced to change our usual methods of doing life and governing our world, we saw the deep fault lines that exist between people, systems, and cultures. In a sick twist of irony, COVID-19 forced us to wear masks while unmasking the ways in which we have failed to serve our neighbors. We saw how paper became more valuable than gold when people bombarded stores to stockpile toilet paper. We heard the cries of Muslim families in places like Sri Lanka when they were unable to perform the last rites for their loved ones taken away by COVID-19 because the government forced cremations, a practice that is condemned in Islam. We saw the deep rifts between private sectors and farmers when the Indian government made laws to modernize agriculture to the detriment of millions of people who rely on their farms for their livelihood. We saw how decades of silence surrounding systemic injustice were shattered when protests erupted all around the world after a white cop suffocated a black man by kneeling on his neck for nine minutes. We saw how politics became pseudo-religions and ideologies became modern-day idols. We saw how people are willing to give up things like decency, empathy, and truth for the sake of protecting their own allegiances.

In the early days of lockdown and quarantine, with empty cups on our shelves and no guests to serve chai to, we began to see why we need to pour and for whom, when, and how. Witnessing how quickly people booked flights to see their families, arranged dinner dates with their friends, or signed up to help with volunteer organizations once the lockdowns were lifted, I like to believe that the pandemic made at least some of us realize that the quality of our lives rests more on the consistency of our pouring than on the intensity of our striving. Being isolated from one another for long periods of time has also helped many of us revisit our assumptions about what constitutes a meaningful existence—that serving others, no strings attached, is arguably the highest gift we can give to others and ourselves.

Albert Camus wrote in *The Plague*, "What's true of all the evils in the world is true of the plague as well. It helps men and women to rise above themselves."[*] At the peak of COVID in 2021, Janik Jayasuriya, an entrepreneur in Sri Lanka, rose above himself when he made weekly trips from Nuwara Eliya to Colombo—a distance of 105 miles (170 kilometers) that took him approximately five to six hours—to donate fresh produce grown from his farms.[†] Moved by the tragic story of a new mom who lost her life to COVID, Ronita Krishna Sharma Rekhi, a mother of a then four-month-old in Assam, India, volunteered to offer breast milk to newborns who had lost their mothers or who were nutritionally deficient.[‡] When Kristin Guerin, an actor in Miami, recov-

---

[*] Albert Camus, *The Plague* (1947), quoted in Nicholas A. Christakis, "Sometimes Altruism Needs to Be Enforced," *Atlantic*, October 20, 2021, https://www.theatlantic.com/ideas/archive/2021/10/pandemic-altruism-selflessness-punishment/620427.

[†] Savani Jayasooriya, "Sri Lankan Entrepreneurs Get Creative during COVID-19," International Finance Corporation, September 2021, https://www.ifc.org/wps/wcm/connect/news_ext_content/ifc_external_corporate_site/news+and+events/news/insights/creativity-of-sri-lankan-entrepreneurs.

[‡] Aastha Ahuja, "Assam Woman Offers to Breastfeed Newborns Who Have Lost Their Mothers to COVID-19," NDTV, July 11, 2021, https://swachhindia.ndtv.com/assam-woman-offers-to-breastfeed-newborns-who-have-lost-their-mothers-to-covid-19-60942.

ered from a severe case of COVID that almost took her life, she and a friend created a network of free community fridges in their area to feed hungry Miamians.* I'm sure there are countless other stories of service during the pandemic that haven't been recorded, stories of individuals who rose beyond the basics of what life required of them in order to pour themselves into others. They remind us that it's often amid the flames of adversity that the shape of mutuality glows. It's often in the waters of collective trauma that the complex flavors of humanity are known.

My bestea, I hope you know that you are destined to serve with love. I hope you recognize that pouring yourself out for your neighbor is not a dissolving of your individuality but an expansion of it. Just as pouring chai elevates the warmth and hospitality experienced in a home, your service elevates the spaces you're in.

So, bestea, make some chai. And, if possible, pour one more cup.

For there's no better way to drink chai than with someone else.

---

* Annie Lowrey, "The Americans Who Knitted Their Own Safety Net," *Atlantic*, March 24, 2021, https://www.theatlantic.com/ideas/archive/2021/03/americans-who -knitted-their-own-safety-net/618377.

CHAPTER 15

taste

Remembering Your Story

Dulce de Leche (Caramel) Chai

Serves 2

INGREDIENTS

1 cup filtered water

½ cup full-fat evaporated milk

3 tablespoons dulce de leche*

1 teaspoon loose leaf Ceylon BOPF black tea

1 teaspoon caramel syrup, plus more to taste

Pinch of salt

METHOD

In a medium pot over medium-high heat, combine the water, evaporated milk, and dulce de leche.

When you see small bubbles on the surface of the milk, stir in the tea and keep aerating it by using a ladle to scoop up the tea and release it back into the pot. You may have to lift the pot a few inches above the flame during this process so that the tea doesn't overflow.

* Caramelized milk or milk "jam." It usually comes in a tin. If you can't find it, there are recipes that tell you how to heat a can of sweetened condensed milk to make your own dulce de leche.

Stir vigorously till all of the dulce de leche dissolves.

When the tea turns a light brown shade, turn the heat off.
Add the caramel syrup.

Strain the tea into a pitcher through a fine-mesh strainer. Aerate the tea by transferring it between the pot and the pitcher a few times, till you see a thick foam appear on the surface of the tea.

If it's not sweet enough, add 1 more teaspoon caramel syrup and keep aerating.

Pour the chai into cups and divide the pinch of salt between them.

Serve and enjoy!

What do I look for in a perfect cup of chai?

After years of making it, and messing up, and trying other chais, I've distilled my expectations down to a four-point C-H-A-I review: Color, Hints of flavor, Aroma, and In-the-mouth feel.

color: Not too dark or too light. Somewhere in the middle. Lighter than milk chocolate. Darker than white chocolate. The color of a Happy Brown Boy™.

hints of flavor: Depends on what chai I'm making. If I make thethani with ginger, I'll be expecting a slight throat burn. If I'm making any chai that involves spices, a good cup will have a subtle astringency, prominent cardamom notes, light clove notes, a ginger kick, and a sweet, milky aftertaste in the mouth.

aroma: This, too, depends on what chai I am making. While hints of flavor are about taste, aroma is mainly about the smell. If I'm making, say, a Pakistani doodh patti chai, I'll be looking for more sweet, caramel notes. If I'm making masala chai or any other chai that has spices added to it, notes of cardamom, ginger, and cinnamon should be evident.

in-the-mouth feel: A very important, yet often overlooked, aspect of chai. A perfect cup of chai will not be too watery or too thick. Even before she tastes it, a good chaiwalli can gauge the texture of the chai by simply sloshing the liquid in her cup to get an idea of its viscosity. This is why aerating chai can also affect its mouthfeel. If I see a few inches of foam in my chai floating above the liquid, I know it's going to be a good cup even without tasting it. If a nonfat milk source or more water is used, you'll end up with little to no foam after aerating it, which is a telltale sign that the chai will feel "thin" in the mouth. The best kinds of chai are those that are slightly less viscous than full-fat milk, that take their time to coat the inside of your mouth with a soft, milky film, and whose flavors still linger in your mouth after gently sloshing down your throat.

There you have it. Look for C-H-A-I when you make your chai.

If you're a chai addict like me, or a connoisseur of anything that requires your senses to assess and parse its quality, you have to rely on the power of your palate memory. This is the list of attributes, qualities, textures, and vocabulary that have been indelibly imprinted on your mind based on the memories you've had of the best versions of this thing. Whether it's a wine sommelier, a third-wave coffee barista, or even a nanni* who is the best biryani maker in the family, they can't do what they do without their memories.

---

* "Grandmother" in Hindi and Urdu.

Tea tasters are no different. Before tea is packaged and shipped out to the market, every batch has to be tasted by a professional tea taster. New technologies and cost-friendly methods, while significantly streamlining the production of chai in large estates, have yet to replace the manual, technical art of tea tasting. Tea tasters on tea estates have to professionally train their senses for at least five years under a master tea taster to learn how to identify the deficiencies in their chai, differentiate one lot of chai from another in the same estate, and classify different types of chai based on their quality for sale at tea auctions.

What does the tea taster look for? Before tasting the tea, the taster will first feel the processed tea between their fingers to test for freshness. Then they might warm the leaves by gently exhaling into the tea in their hands so that they can assess the notes from its aroma. Meanwhile, an assistant "tea boy" will prepare a long table with five-ounce cups arranged in single file. He will then add approximately three grams of each variety of tea that needs to be tested into each cup. Not long after that, another tea assistant will arrive with a pot of water that has come to a full boil and will add water to each cup. While this is happening, the taster will look for the "agony," or the gentle unfolding of the tea leaves, in the cup in order to assess the visual appearance of the infused leaf. After years of doing this, tea tasters are well versed in every shade of color between black and deep brown and can not only pinpoint the possible causes for the coloration but also identify preventive actions for each undesired shade.

Then comes the actual tasting. The taster will take in a few sips, making distinctly loud noises as they slosh the tea around with their tongue to coat every part of the mouth, before spitting it out into a special spittoon typically held in the left hand. While "politely" sipping tea might provide less than 50 percent of the sensory resolution, aerating the olfactory bulb with a combination of inhaled air and rapid liquid movement allows the tea taster to taste with their *brain*, using the entirety of their senses and memory palate to assess its qualities. After spitting out the tea, they will then sound off words, which to the untrained ear may sound like gibberish but to their assistant are important descriptors of the tea that will be used to determine the next stage of the manufacturing process:

Stylish to describe the quality of the leaf.

Bright to describe the overall quality of the tea.

Strong to refer to the "body" of the tea, the depth or the lack thereof of the liquor.

Sour, dry, spicy, fruity, malty, and *smoky* to describe the flavor notes of the tea.

Coppery, dull, or *light* for color.

Tea tasters remind us that good chai is not just a memorable product but a product of memory. Infused in your chai—whether it's Assam CTC, Darjeeling, Kenyan BOP, or Ceylon BOPF—are not only the flavors from its terroir, the heritage of its tea estate, and the perseverance of the tea pluckers but also a wonderfully complex distillation of the memories of the best chai experiences. With every sip, you taste history. You taste story.

You, too, my bestea, are a masterpiece of memory. Whether you realize it or not, your reflections, recollections, and memories continue to reinforce your identity and shape the person you're becoming. To put it another way, you are what you remember. A common misconception is that we are what happens to us, that our characters are altered by the joys and traumas we have experienced in the past. But a more nuanced understanding of our pasts and their effects on us would suggest that the ways we remember the past anew are what ultimately affect the trajectory of our lives.

Life doesn't just happen to us. We happen to our lives. And life responds back. That's why our perception of ourselves and our perception of others are inextricably connected to what we choose to remember.

Choose a period of your life that was particularly hard or challenging. What do you remember from that time? What memories jump out from the recesses of your mind? For me, it was the time between January 2020 and January 2022. I remember the disorientation I felt after the tragic death of my favorite basketball player, Kobe Bean Bryant. I remember the first time I got a COVID test—the instant cough and tears induced by the deepest swab I'd ever felt tickle my brain through my nose. I recall the first day we did church outside. I remember the hospital visits. I remember the funerals. I remember sitting cross-legged with families in silence on their house floor less than twenty-four hours after the death of their loved one. I remember making chai for my parents, who visited us from Sri

Lanka. I remember saying yet another tearful goodbye to them at the airport that opened up old wounds from memories of leaving home. I remember breaking down on the shoulders of a man I'd never met before because of his unexpected kindness toward my parents at LAX.* I remember seeing Khayali's firstborn—my first nephew, Zion John—during a FaceTime call with her at the hospital. I remember simultaneously experiencing extreme joy and sharp pain at seeing Zion but not being able to go to Sri Lanka so Kevin Māma† could hug him in person. I remember laughing with Elynn. I remember crying with her. I remember being furious at God. I remember being at peace with God.

But even with these time stamps on my memory, the pandemic has not only made it difficult to construct a coherent narrative around these events but it has also made it harder to connect these memories to the rest of our lives. You might have suffered for your loved ones who got COVID. You might have had to fight it yourself. Your employer might have let you go, and you might have struggled to make ends meet. Add to this the fears stemming from uncertain futures, unreliable governments, and unpredictable circumstances. The anxieties from these stressors inhibit our abilities to open up our beings to create new memories and connect old ones.

So, first, I see you. If you're anything like me, in order to sur-

---

* The Los Angeles International Airport, i.e., the purgatory of the airport world.

† "Uncle" in Tamil; his mom's brother.

vive, you have overvalued your ability to heal and undervalued your ability to hope. You have overestimated your abilities to fix, resolve, and thrive and underestimated your abilities to dream, accept, and be.

Second, I believe in you. I believe in us. As long as you have breath in your lungs and even the smallest ember of hope for a better future quietly glowing in your heart, you still have the ability to create new memories and construct new stories. You have the capability of drawing new lines of continuity between your pre-pandemic and post-pandemic life so that this season feels less like a definitive end of a story and more like a new chapter.

What practices help you remember? Making chai helps me remember who I am by reconnecting me to my roots. The aroma, the astringency, and the aeration of chai transport me to the people and the places that have made me. Making tea for others reinforces values like hospitality and generosity that were passed on to me by my ancestors. The entire process, from beginning to end, activates a matrix of memories at the core of my person, relocating my story—even for a moment—from the rat race of achievement and significance to an ancient history of resilience.

Journaling is another habit that I've cultivated over the last few years, which, unsurprisingly, has helped to cultivate me. I've put the best statement I recall from my youth pastor—"The shortest pencil is longer than the longest memory"—into practice by taking a few minutes each day to record key "aha" moments and things I want to remember, so I can discern the unforced rhythms of Grace moving through my life. This practice has also helped me realize that the extent to which I can remember my past is the extent to which I can receive the present and reimagine the future.

So imagine with me a decade into the future.

What story are you going to tell about challenging moments in your life? To your children, your grandchildren, or your loved ones, years after the pandemic has become a blip in our collective history? How are you going to remember the events of this time in years to come?

Because, bestea, just as the memories of the tea tasters inform their practice and ensure the production of the best-quality chai, the way you remember key moments of your life today—in all their beauty or brutality—will transform into lessons that will rescue someone else tomorrow.

Even if that someone is you.

CHAPTER 16

grounds

Journeying through Grief

Kevin's Signature Chai

Serves 2

INGREDIENTS

4 green cardamom pods

1 (2-inch) cinnamon stick

½ cup filtered water

1½ teaspoons loose leaf Ceylon BOPF black tea

½ cup full-fat milk

½ cup full-fat evaporated milk

1 teaspoon fresh crushed ginger

4 tablespoons sweetened condensed milk

Pinch of salt

METHOD

Crush the cardamom and cinnamon with a mortar and pestle and set aside.

In a medium pot, heat the water over medium heat.

When you see small bubbles at the bottom of the pot, add the tea.

When the water comes to a boil, keep stirring and aerating for 30 seconds. Then add the full-fat milk and evaporated milk.

Add the crushed spices and ginger. Stir.

When the tea rises to the top of the pot, turn the heat off.

Pour the sweetened condensed milk into a pitcher. Strain the tea into the pitcher through a fine-mesh strainer. Stir vigorously so that all the condensed milk dissolves completely.

Aerate the tea by transferring it between the pot and the pitcher a few times or by using an electric frother, till you see a foam appearing on the surface of the tea.

Pour the chai into cups and divide the pinch of salt between them.

Serve and enjoy!

Your chai experience doesn't need to end after you finish your cup.

Tea grounds are rich in nutrients and tannic acid, which, when added to the soil of plants that require lower pH levels and high acidity, can improve the quality of their growth. So after you're done with your chai, if your tea grounds are still in the strainer, don't discard them in the trash. First, rinse them to get rid of any milk solids and sugar because they can contaminate the soil. Then recycle them. Tea grounds are usually used to nourish plants in one of two ways: You can add them as mulch to your topsoil, which will form a protective layer against excess heat and moisten the soil while attracting earthworms and other critters that will heighten soil quality. You can also incorporate tea grounds into your compost, which will hasten the decomposition process and increase the amount of nutrients in your soil.

This reincarnation of chai as fertilizer, adding life to plants and improving the ecosystem even after it has accomplished its main function, reminds me of those who, even if they are no longer with us, continue to enrich our lives with meaning.

Recently, for me, that was my friend Mark.

It was a beautiful Sunday morning in Oceanside, in San Diego County. Eddie, the senior pastor of our church and my colleague in ministry, and I drove to visit the Cochrans. Mark, Vonnie, and their adult children—Chynna, Chapman, Chance, and Chelsea—had been a core part of our congregation for decades, infusing life into our community with their vivaciousness, energy, and sheer love for life.

They are usually the life of the party. But today, it was different.

After a long fight with cancer, Mark had passed away the previous night, while surrounded by his loved ones in their home. Their home—usually filled with the sounds of laughter and the tantrums of their grandchildren—was thick with grief, made evident by the broken welcomes of their children as we entered their living room.

We hugged, our embraces tighter and longer than usual. We reminisced. We laughed. Small talk punctuated with long silences and stifled tears helped pass the time until Chapman, the third oldest and father of three-year-old Koa, reached out to me with something in his hand.

"Bro, have you heard about this?" Chapman said, showing me a beautifully designed cylindrical canister with a lid.

I smiled. The words on the canister read "Fresh, Original Masala Chai."

"It's not coming out as good as I thought it would, so maybe we're doing it wrong?" Chapman said with a bit of anticipation.

I opened the canister to inspect its contents. It was a dark, fragrant, sticky chai mix, which, according to the instructions, didn't require anything more than water, some type of thick milk, and heat to transform it into chai.

"This doesn't look terrible," I responded with some hopefulness. "If anything, it's still going to be a few notches above your Starbucks 'chai tea latte.'"

It felt good to see him struggle to hide a chuckle.

Then his eyes lit up. "You want to make it right now?" Chap asked eagerly.

I wasn't sure I had heard him right. *Is this acceptable? I thought. Won't this be some kind of mourning etiquette violation? I'm supposed to be sitting with the family and listening to stories, not making chai! Also, there's like . . . eleven people in this house I'd have to make chai for! Will we have enough for all?* The reasons to politely refuse kept mounting—until I realized that to say no would probably come across as rejection instead of propriety.

So I got to work.

Heat on. Pot. Milk. Sticky chai. First rise. Second rise. Heat off. Sugar. Taste. Adjust sweetness. Mix. Strain. Aerate. Pour.

There was enough for everyone and then some.

I never get tired of people's reactions to their first sip of some good masala chai. Little do they realize that they are about to embark on a sensory journey. Even before you taste it, you're going to smell it. The sweet, cinnamony steam gently caresses your face as you move the cup toward your lips. At that first sip, lightly cooled from the air you just squeezed between your teeth so that your mouth doesn't burn, chai sloshes around in your mouth, coating all parts of your tongue and flooding your brain with so many sensations that you're wonderfully disoriented for a moment. You don't realize that your eyebrows are raised. Your mind lets out an inaudible *whoa*. Like a surprise visit from a group of friends you haven't seen in a while, the ginger and the spices show up at the front door of your being as the chai hits the back of your throat. It's a gathering. It makes sense. You don't want it to end, but as you swallow, the sip nudges your limbic system to prepare you for the next gathering about to take place.

There are few things that remind you of your aliveness like a sip of homemade chai.

And I think that's what the Cochran clan felt that morning, even for a brief moment. They were reminded that not everything was gone. Jolted into reality by new flavors, they realized that they could still taste. They could still smell. In the midst of unbearable grief, each sip permitted them reentry into reality as they regained some energy, not necessarily to move *on*, but just enough to move *through*.

In November 2016, I was staying at a small cabin in Yosemite Valley with my friends Logan and Makenzy when I received a Facebook message from Khayali, asking me to call home. By her tone, I knew this was urgent. I immediately called home, and Amma answered with a broken "Hi, Kevin."

I wasn't ready for the next few words that came out of her:

"Kevin . . . Paatti died."

I'd preached about grief before. I'd done funerals for others before. But I didn't know what grief really meant until I lost my grandmother. My body froze. My stomach tightened. I felt nauseated and was about to throw up. I had no words, but short, inaudible, half-formed breaths escaped my mouth as if someone had punched my lungs from the inside. My legs gave away as I crumpled to the floor. My eyes hurt, but there were no tears. Maybe that was when God thought it necessary to open the tear reservoirs of my being that had been closed up to that point, because eventually they all came out, flooding my face and spilling over onto my phone screen.

I had already known Paatti was not doing well, and I was counting the days until I would get to see her. When I told Amma that I was going to book a ticket to come to Sri Lanka for Paatti's funeral, she sternly refused. She told me that she was not ready to see me only for a few days, just to say another goodbye. I reluctantly agreed. Realizing that I would not be able to travel to Sri Lanka to be with my family and to grieve with them shattered my world. I felt evicted from my own reality. Nothing could have prepared me for the disorientation I'd feel for the next few weeks and months. To me, Paatti could do no wrong. She was the person I thought of when I pictured unconditional love and acceptance. She was one of the few humans in my life with whom I'd never felt that I had to prove my worth in order to be loved. So losing her felt like losing a human-shaped tapestry of love, ripped apart from my inner being.

It's been seven years since Paatti died. Going through this experience has shown me that grief is not a state of mind as much as it's a way of being. Grief affects us at a subterranean level, making impressions on our souls that last a lifetime, and it cannot be reduced to a mental disposition or a set of painful emotions. Perhaps grieving is a journey of reframing our pains, reorienting our loves, and reimagining new futures without the people we love—an excruciating process that re-forms our lives, somehow enlarging our capacities to feel more, live more, and love more.

Though the initial shock has subsided and the tears are more intermittent, it's taken a while for me to find the words to articulate the emotions and sensations I felt during those first few weeks of slowly realizing that I was not going to see Paatti's radiating smile at the front porch, welcoming me to our house. I would no longer feel the warmth of her thick skin on mine, or her rough, calloused hands on my face, nor smell the faint vethalai,* paakku,† and sunnambu‡ odor from her breath when she called me by my name. But these memories have changed my life in ways that I could not describe to you even if I tried. I don't know if I've become a better person for reliving these moments, but I know I'm a different one.

I have since accepted that grief is going to be an endless journey. Unlike other trips that have a clear beginning and an end, a memory or a feeling can suddenly whisk you into grief without warning you. You are forced to travel on this road for a while, until you decide to get off, albeit temporarily, so that you can face reality again. More "locations" are added to this journey with every person in your life who has passed on. I've come to

---

* Betel leaf, a common stimulant in many parts of South Asia.

† Areca nut, chewed with betel leaves to heighten awareness and warm the body.

‡ Slaked lime, made by adding water to quicklime and used as a paste along with betel leaves and areca nut as a stimulant.

understand that this process is catalyzed not just by people who are no longer here with us, but also by those who are no longer who we remember them to be. Visiting my relatives in Sri Lanka after living in the States for the past decade, I've found that the excitement of seeing familiar faces after a long time is tainted by a quiet realization that these people have changed, and that I have changed as well. Maybe to grieve is to keep remembering, the continual act of reattaching ourselves to our loved ones vis-à-vis our memories of them—which means that at every stage of our existence, we are never truly alone.

I used to think that grief was the opposite of joy. But now, re-playing the memories of Paatti, Thaatha, Mark, and others I've grieved, I wonder if grief is not necessarily the absence of joy but rather its strongest memory. Maybe the joy never left. Maybe upon the departure of loved ones, joy transforms into something more alive, more solid yet malleable—like lava—galvanizing the depths of our being with their memories such that our life becomes an amalgam of theirs. I felt no joy when they were gone. As I write these words, however, I realize how much joy I feel for having loved them and having been loved by them.

The depths of my pain from losing the people I've loved reveal the breadth of my capacity to pour love. Even if I wanted to, I can't stop missing Paatti. I cannot choose to stop grieving Thaatha. When I think about Mark, my being goes into a different mode without any warning. Grieving has helped me realize the terrifyingly beautiful truth that my love for others can, in fact, transcend the categories I use to understand or constrain them, that the intensity of my care can be stronger than the rationalizations of my logic. Grief has sensitized me to the magic of the mundane, the beauty of life, the miracle of perception, and the joy of relationships. I can never take anything for granted.

My bestea, as you remember your loved ones who have passed, I hope your lips curve into a smile at their memory before your eyes fill with tears.

I hope you know that the detours of death and loss can be vista points that reveal new landscapes in your current reality, new vantages to view your life and the lives of others.

Like chai grounds nourishing your potted plants, I hope you realize that endings can lead to new beginnings.

That even in death, life is beautiful.

CHAPTER 17

conclusion

Brewing in Community

Can you remember your best cup of chai?

I remember mine like it was yesterday.

July 14, 2017. It had been just five days since Elynn and I had said "I do" to each other during our wedding in Sri Lanka. We were now at the Madulkelle Tea and Eco Lodge, spending our honeymoon in our own private yurt situated among cloud forests. The views of the tea plantations from our location were stunning. Sunrays refracting through the gentle morning mists painted the landscape with soothing shades of green. The afternoon air was dewy, infused with my favorite smell of petrichor emanating from the rain-soaked soil.

That morning, we walked over to the main lodge, where an array of Sri Lankan and Western delectables were being served. It was there that we were introduced to Ajith—a forty-something, gentle man with a kind smile—who was our server. He asked us if we wanted something to drink before our meal, to which both of us said in unison, "Tea, please!" A few minutes later, Ajith arrived with two cups of tea—one without dairy for Elynn and a regular one for me. He promptly left to attend to the other guests and to give us some time to decide on our order.

When I looked at the tea, I knew it was going to be good. The color was just right. A good bit of foam on the top. The aromatic steam warmed our faces. I took a sip.

Oh.

My.

Goodness.

I've had thethani for as long as I can remember. But never like this.

I almost jumped out of my chair when Ajith came back to get our order. I begged him to tell me how he made it. With his shy but surprised disposition, typical of servers in boutique hotels who are approached by "suddhas"* with questions, Ajith described how he used the BOPF tea dust from the Madulkelle estate, made a roux from full-fat milk powder and sugar, poured the strained tea into that mix, aerated it a few times, and then poured it into an ornate porcelain cup.

No. It's too simple, I thought. *He's hiding a secret technique or ingredient. There's no way.*

After badgering him for more details, I was disappointed when Ajith told me that that was it. Because his process was very similar to how I usually make my own Lankan tea, I wondered if it was maybe the quality of the local Madulkelle tea. Maybe it was the type of sugar he used? Maybe it was his hardware? But there was nothing new about Ajith's technique that I hadn't done before.

The more I savored the tea, wishing this experience would never end, the more I realized something else that I might have

---

* "Foreigners," or more specifically "whites." While I'm too melanated to be considered one, the fact that I'm married to Elynn, an American, in addition to my broken Sinhala, might have caused Ajith to put me in this category.

missed in my investigation. It wasn't a method or a technique. It wasn't the tea. It wasn't the ingredients.

It wasn't just how it had been made.

It was who I was having it with.

This was the first time I was sharing tea with Elynn as her husband.

After knowing her for eight years, dating long distance for more than four years, enduring all sorts of ups and downs in our relationship, and learning to appreciate our cultural differences and their blessings, sharing this chai with my life partner felt surreal and extraordinary—like arriving at an oasis that we missed on the map because we were too focused on survival. When you're at the brink, choosing next steps over best steps, prioritizing endurance over enjoyment, the things that are supposed to simply sustain you end up being the things that transform you.

For the hungry, food becomes sacred.

For the thirsty, drink becomes spiritual.

On that beautiful morning, as the realization that we were never going to say goodbye slowly settled in, perhaps more capacity in my being opened up, activating sensory receptors that might have been dormant until that moment. In the presence of loving community, a simple milk tea transformed itself into a muse that unlocked a new era of meaning in our lives.

Chai reminds us that while a good brew can flavor your senses, good community can flavor your life. It also reminds us that while all of us attempt to make ourselves, none of us are really "self-made." I am who I am because of the communities I've been a part of. You are who you are because of the people you have shared your life with—whether they are people who've had your best interests at heart or those who have imposed their stories onto you. Our characters are ultimately a reaction to, and a conglomeration of, our communities.

But in order to realize the importance of community, to truly understand the value of the people who have nurtured your life, you must first recognize the sacredness of your story. This is ultimately why I put pen to paper to write this book and invite you into my home for chai—to help you, my bestea, remember, even for a moment, why your story particularly matters in this ongoing, unfolding history of our collective humanity.

The terroir of chai is a meditation on the significance of your character. It's a reminder that you are not an isolated island but a continent—nourishing, and being nourished by, the world around you.

The leaves of chai remind you of your capacity for empathy, to understand and love the "other."

The labor that went into making your chai is a reminder that gratitude is not a passive mood that exists purely as a kind of "consciousness," but an active mode that aligns with your moral bent toward justice.

The drying process of chai reminds you that the liminal spaces you find yourself in are not limited spaces but limitless spaces where your being is sensitized to new possibilities for flourishing.

The recipes of chai show you that you can achieve true mastery not only by pursuing a love of habits but by cultivating habits of love.

The thirst satiated, and created, by chai is a meditation on the depth of your desires and the breadth of their impact.

The crushing of the spices reminds you that although the painful experiences of your life have broken you in different places, you, bestea, are not broken.

The cup that holds your chai signifies that the best kind of life is not lived by pursuing unrestricted purpose but by incorporating purposeful constraints.

The heat that made your chai is a reminder of how your attention has shaped, and continues to shape, your story.

The boiling process of chai reminds you that your story is in progress. That you are not worthless. You are just steeping.

The wait for chai shows you the importance of rest—a reminder that you are not a human "doing" but a human being.

The foam on top of your chai that comes as a result of aeration represents the enduring nature of your identity despite its displacements and disorientations.

The pouring of chai reminds you that the flavors of your story are best realized when you pour yourself into others through service.

The first taste of your chai reminds you of the value of your memories and how they can help you face the challenges of your future.

The filtered grounds of chai can remind you that grief is but love that is yearning for home, that the brutality of death can co-exist with the possibility of new hope.

I wipe my pot dry, tap the water out of my strainer, and put them away. I close the lid of my dollar-store pickle jar where I store my Ceylon BOPF and place it next to my other tea supplies. I close the Ziploc bags with whole cinnamon and cardamom and place them back in my freezer. I see Leo and Phoebe cuddled up on their cat tree next to my fiddle-leaf fig tree, basking in the dusky sunset glow.

I sit down on my gray IKEA couch. I don't know where my phone is, but I don't worry about it. At least not right now. Because I am here. And I want to be.

I realize that no amount of chai can replace the beauty of the time we've shared together. The intertwining of our stories, even for a brief moment, even if it's through these pages, has changed our lives forever. Because you, bestea, have blessed me with the gifts of your time and perspective. So, from the bottom of my heart, thank you.

Thank you for coming to my home.

Thank you for thinking with me.

Thank you for your resonance and your dissonance with what I've said.

But most of all, thank you for being you.

There is an ancient concept called Atithi Devo Bhava, a Hindu-Buddhist philosophy describing the holiness of the host-guest relationship. "Atithi" refers to someone who does not have a calendrical sense of time, or one who visits anytime. "Devo" means "God," and "Bhava" means "to be." Found in the Taittirīya Upanishad, this phrase in its immediate literary context translates to "You become the one who considers that guests are equivalent to God." If you have been to India, or have been invited into the home of a Hindu family in the diaspora, it won't be long before you realize how foundational this philosophy is within the culture.

When they share chai with you, you are not merely a guest.

You become a god.

As you sip your chai today, may it remind you that your story is neither an afterthought nor an anecdote but a saga—a multicolored tapestry of tales representing a genealogy of difficulties, joys, and hopes, all tied together by a single thread of courage, bonded by the thick adhesive of relationships, and held together by a single cup.

So I look forward to hearing from you. Let me know when you try out a recipe. There are fifteen different recipes to plunge you into the world of chai.

And fifteen different entry points to the way of chai.

You're already on it, bestea. But the journey has just begun.

Talk to you soon.

Your favorite chaiwalla,

kevin

acknowledgments

This is my first book.

There's no way I could have written that sentence without the following people, without whom this would not be in your hands right now.

Usually authors save the best accolades for last. But just in case this might be the only paragraph you'll read on this page, I'm going to start with the most important: my best friend and wife, Elynn. Thank you for believing in me when I didn't have the courage to, sweetheart. You've been nothing but a consistent support throughout this journey. Every inch of my creativity has your fingerprints on it. I love you so much, mi amor. Both chai and life have become sweeter since I met you.

To my editors—Sara Carder and Joanna Ng at TarcherPerigee, and Kimberley Lim: If it was ever possible to transform stale tea leaves into a fine-tasting chai, that's what you did with this book. You took my scraps and turned them into magic. Thank you for being patient with my last-minute turnarounds, run-on sentences, and incoherent arguments. Y'all are wizards. To Carla Iannone, Abby Stubenhofer, Rachel Dugan, Farin Schlussel, Casey Maloney, Marian Lizzi, Lindsay Gordon, Megan Newman, and the rest of the publishing team: Thank you for taking a chance on this first-time author. Thank you for creating space to share these often under-represented stories from the South Asian experience with the rest of the world.

To Jeff Boyd: It takes a certain type of boss to not only take a chance on hiring a scattered, multipotential, often-confused person like me, but also affirm and validate their interests outside of their nine-to-five. Thank you for your wisdom, quiet strength, and exemplary leadership.

To Deepa Bharath: You were one of the first journalists to write a piece on me that went beyond discussing my TikTok fame and into my philosophies on life. That piece opened many doors for me.

To Lynn Johnston, my literary agent: You reached out to me when I didn't even know who, or what, a literary agent was. I will always remember that first Zoom call when you asked me about my story, after which you told me that I had a book waiting to be unleashed. Thank you for introducing and orienting me to the world of publishing and book writing. Thank you for believing in my story.

To my professors at Andrews University: I failed high school literature. But y'all took in a scared, insecure, eighteen-year-old Sri Lankan kid, taught him how to fall in love with reading, learning, and cross-cultural communication, and made him realize that his life is not a mistake but his greatest superpower. You helped me reconstruct my faith. You taught me how to be a world changer.

To my Oceanside SDA Church community: You received Elynn and me with open arms right after seminary and gave us some of the best five years of our lives. I'd run out of page space if I were to mention every single one of you. Thank you for teaching me how to be a pastor. Thank you for trusting me with your high schoolers and young adults. Thank you for the memories, relationships, tears, and laughter. I can't wait to have an International Food Festival in the Kingdom with all of you.

To the familia of my in-laws, Elvin (Dad), Linette (Mom), Naty (Sister), Witito (Grandpa), and Tata (Grandma): I didn't know what receiving or giving affirmations meant until I met y'all. Thank you for your consistent encouragement, words of counsel, and being some of my greatest cheerleaders throughout this journey. Only second to knowing Christ, the greatest gift of God to me has been your family.

To my besteas: You've been part of this tribe for way longer than you needed to. Thank you for your wisdom, friendship, interest, and willingness to journey together. You've changed our lives.

To Wilson (Dada), Pari (Amma), Khayali (Sister), Zion (Nephew), Andrew (Brother-in-Law), and the rest of the fam-bam in the motherland: This book is for you. For us. None of these ideas and stories would have existed if not for the choices you made to continue our legacy. I know I made you proud.

And, reader, if you haven't heard it from your own appa, amma, thaatha, or paatti, hear me loud and clear:

I am proud of you.

references

Ahuja, Aastha. "Assam Woman Offers to Breastfeed Newborns Who Have Lost Their Mothers to COVID-19." NDTV, July 11, 2021, https://swachhindia.ndtv.com/assam-woman-offers-to-breastfeed-newborns-who-have-lost-their-mothers-to-covid-19-60942.

Bernard, Sara. "Neuroplasticity: Learning Physically Changes the Brain." Edutopia, December 1, 2010, https://www.edutopia.org/neuroscience-brain-based-learning-neuroplasticity.

Chatterjee, Piya. *A Time for Tea: Women, Labor and Post/Colonial Politics on an Indian Plantation.* New Delhi: Zubaan, 2003.

Christakis, Nicholas A. "Sometimes Altruism Needs to Be Enforced." *The Atlantic*, October 20, 2021, https://www.theatlantic.com/ideas/archive/2021/10/pandemic-altruism-selflessness-punishment/620427.

Heiss, Mary Lou, and Robert J. Heiss. *The Story of Tea: A Cultural History and Drinking Guide.* Berkeley, CA: Ten Speed Press, 2007.

Heschel, Abraham Joshua. *The Sabbath: Its Meaning for Modern Man.* New York: Farrar, Straus and Giroux, 1951.

Hwee Hwee, Tan. "In Search of the Lotus Land." *Quarterly Literary Review Singapore* 1, no. 1 (October 2001), http://www.qlrs.com/issues/oct2001/essays/lotusland.html.

International Movement against All Forms of Discrimination and Racism. *Racial Discrimination in Sri Lanka.* UN Committee on the Elimination of Racial Discrimination, July 2016, https://imadr.org/wordpress/wp-content/uploads/2016/07/IMADR_Sri-Lanka_CERD90_July2016.pdf.

Jayasooriya, Savani. "Sri Lankan Entrepreneurs Get Creative during COVID-19." International Finance Corporation, September 2021, https://www.ifc.org/wps/wcm/connect/news_ext_content/ifc_external _corporate_sitenews+and+events/news/insights/creativity-of-sri-lankan -entrepreneurs.

Keyes, Corey L. "The Mental Health Continuum: From Languishing to Flourishing in Life." *Journal of Health and Social Behavior* 43, no. 2 (June 2002): 207–22, https://doi.org/10.2307/3090197.

King, Martin Luther, Jr. "Remaining Awake through a Great Revolution." Commencement address, Oberlin College, June 1965, https://www2 .oberlin.edu/external/eog/blackhistorymonth/mlk/commaddress.html.

Lowe, Lisa. *The Intimacies of Four Continents.* Durham, NC: Duke University Press, 2015.

Lowrey, Annie. "The Americans Who Knitted Their Own Safety Net." *The Atlantic*, March 24, 2021, https://www.theatlantic.com/ideas/archive /2021/03/americans-who-knitted-their-own-safety-net/618377.

Rajbangshi, Preety R., and Devaki Nambiar. "'Who Will Stand Up for Us?' The Social Determinants of Health of Women Tea Plantation Workers in India." *International Journal for Equity in Health* 19, no. 29 (2020), https://doi.org/10.1186/s12939-020-1147-3.

Rappaport, Erika Diane. *A Thirst for Empire: How Tea Shaped the Modern World.* Princeton, NJ: Princeton University Press, 2017.

Shipper, Dan, Clarissa Ong, and Michael Twohig. "Perfectionism: Why and How to Beat It." Every Media, May 28, 2022, https://every.to /superorganizers/perfectionism-why-and-how-to-beat-it.

Simon, Richard, and Dominic Sansoni. *Ceylon Tea: The Trade That Made a Nation.* Colombo, Sri Lanka: Colombo Tea Traders' Association, 2017.

Smith, James K. A. *You Are What You Love: The Spiritual Power of Habit.* Grand Rapids, MI: Brazos Press, 2016.

Soon, Edwin. *The Dilmah Way of Tea.* Peliyagoda, Sri Lanka: Ceylon Tea Services, 2009.

about the author

Kevin Wilson nurtures a growing community of half a million chai-loving humans on TikTok and Instagram (@CrossCultureKev) by using chai, the cherished drink of his Sri Lankan family, as a medium for storytelling. A third culture kid who has lived in or visited fifteen countries, Wilson knows what it means to be a cultural outsider. He is a digital/social media coordinator for Andrews University—his alma mater—and also an ordained minister in the Seventh-day Adventist Church with a decade of pastoral ministry experience. He currently lives in Berrien Springs, Michigan, with his wife, Elynn, and two fur children, Phoebe and Leo.